This book of amusing parables from Don Farber's life as a literary agent and show business lawyer is a celebration of practical nice manners and tough-minded decency in the process of achieving equitable agreements in all sorts of businesses, and even in social situations where sanity has a chance to prevail.

—**KURT VONNEGUT**, author of *Slaughterhouse Five*

Donald Farber has produced a gem. Although, as he concedes, it is impossible to take a pill and gain common sense or grace, his book provides a thoughtful and concise checklist of what every good negotiator should consider in entering into and conducting negotiations. It may be better to be smart than stupid, shrewd rather than naive, but ultimately the common sense approach will prevail. Mr. Farber's book is a handy reference that should be on every negotiator's desk.

—**LEE C. WHITE**, Assistant Special Counsel to President John F. Kennedy, Counsel to President Johnson, former Chairman, Federal Power Commission

Cheers for Don Farber, who with grace and skill demystifies the process of negotiating, among the most familiar but frequently intimidating of human relationships. *Common Sense Negotiation* provides a handy guide for the amateur as well as the professional, and it does so with consideration for feelings as well as rights, money and other negotiable things.

—**SIDNEY OFFIT**, author of *Memoir of the Bookie's Son*

Regrettably, common sense is often an uncommon characteristic of those engaged in deal making. Don Farber not only argues for common sense but in an engaging and accessible style describes what it means! To acknowledge that in most negotiations the outcome should be win-win rather than zero sum may startle some people but in entertaining examples he powerfully demonstrates the point.

—**HARVEY PERLMAN**, Dean, University of Nebraska College of Law

COMMON SENSE NEGOTIATION

THE ART OF
WINNING
GRACEFULLY

BY
DONALD C. FARBER

BAY PRESS

Printed in the United States of America.

Bay Press, Inc.
115 West Denny Way
Seattle, WA 98119-4205
Fax: 206.284.1218

Cover and interior design: Philip Kovacevich
Cover artist: Isabel Kahn

Library of Congress Cataloguing-in-Publication Data

Farber, Donald C.
        Common Sense Negotiation : the art of winning gracefully /
        by Donald C. Farber
                p. cm.
        (alk. paper)
        ISBN 0-941920-38-0
        ISBN 0-941920-45-3 (pbk)
        1. Negotiation in business. 2. Deals. I. Title
HD58.6.F37   1996
658.4--dc20   95-52182
                                                        CIP

With great love

for my dear, beautiful grandchildren,

Miranda and Justin,

with whom I have had many negotiations

and never won a single one

CONTENTS

PREFACE

This book is about negotiating a deal—not just any deal, but one that satisfies all of the parties. In these pages I plan to share the techniques and tactics that have worked for me in achieving this kind of deal, and that will work for you, too, helping you to negotiate intelligently and win gracefully.

"Winning," by my definition, means getting as much as you ought to—neither taking advantage of someone nor settling for less than you're entitled. It means achieving a good contract which, simply put, is a legally enforceable agreement and, by my definition, is synonymous with a good deal. "Gracefully," in this context, means convincing the other party that what you are asking for is in his or her best interests, that you have a community of interest rather than a conflict of interest, and that you end up respecting each other no matter how much you may have disagreed in the beginning.

This book won't teach you how to convince a computer salesman to sell you a $3,500 computer for $2,500, how to beat your mother-in-law at bridge or how to persuade your offspring that they should go to a particular college. (It won't even help convince them to go to college.) I'm not focusing here on the one-time-only sort of negotiation. Instead, my aim is to help you create and maintain, within the framework of the deal, a constructive relationship with a person or persons with whom you plan to work over the long term.

Since I am an attorney in the entertainment industry, most of the examples in this book will relate to "show biz" and authors and stars, but the principles set forth are applicable to any business negotiation that involves creating a healthy and lasting relationship between the parties to a deal.

Through the years I myself have enjoyed and helped my clients to enjoy hundreds of such relationships, resulting from thousands of negotiations and countless good deals. In my forty-five-year career I have been privileged to represent or be closely associated with a lot of well-known people, among them novelists Kurt Vonnegut (*Slaughterhouse Five*) and John D. MacDonald (the Travis McGee suspense series); character actor Kevin McCarthy (*Invasion of the Body Snatchers*); television personality Geraldo Rivera; movie star Geraldine Fitzgerald (*Wuthering Heights*, with Oberon and Olivier); actress Lucie Arnaz, daughter of Lucille Ball and Desi Arnaz, and her actor-husband Larry Luckinbill; actress Olympia Dukakis (*Moonstruck*) and her actor-husband Louis Zorich; actress Lynn Redgrave, daughter of Sir Michael and sister of Vanessa, and her director-husband John Clark; character actress Estelle Parsons (*Bonnie and Clyde*); jazz legend Duke Ellington; movie star Joan Bennett (*Little Women*); stage actress Carol Shelley (*Showboat*); television actresses Bonnie Franklin ("One Day at a Time") and Rosetta Le Noire ("Family Matters"); actress (and character!) Tallulah Bankhead and her Shakespearean actor-husband John Emery; prima ballerina Tamara Geva (George Balanchine's first wife); jazz singer Yolande Bavan (who replaced Annie Ross in the trio Lambert, Hendricks & Ross); everyone associated with the original off-Broadway production of *The Fantasticks*, written by Tom Jones and Harvey Schmidt; magicians Ricky Jay and Doug Henning; The Actors' Studio (where Marlon

Brando, Paul Newman and Montgomery Clift, among others, studied); and the Stratford Shakespearean Festival Foundation of Canada (the most prestigious repertory theater on this continent).

It has been, and still is, so much fun, I envy me!

ACKNOWLEDGMENTS

This may seem strange, but without the inspiration of some weasel brains (there are not too many, fortunately, in my business), this book never would have been written. So I have to acknowledge and thank those nitpickers, those hagglers, those quibblers, those greedy lamebrains, those squabblers and those bickerers who made me miserable during some needlessly lengthy negotiations because they didn't know what they were doing. It was with their help that I realized how *not* to negotiate and the importance of doing it right. So, thanks a bunch.

But even more sincere thanks go to those truly professional attorneys, agents, managers and representatives who acted in a responsible manner, not trying to get an unfair edge, but helping to fashion an agreement that would work for and be fair to all the parties concerned.

Every author should enjoy the privilege of having editors and publishers like Sally Brunsman, Kim Barnett, and Paula Ladenburg. They are intelligent, sensitive, caring and smart. I thank them.

Of course, love and thanks go to my family who tolerated my repeated, temporary isolations to get this book done. My beautiful grandchildren, Miranda and Justin, my lovely daughter Pat and her husband Nef, my brilliant son Seth and his good friend Dina, and my everloving, wonderful wife Annie have my love, my appreciation and thanks.

SETTING THE STAGE

It all starts with The Offer—the "invitation to the dance." You approach someone or they approach you, and a dialogue—the negotiation—begins, with one party offering to do something for the other party or requesting that the other party do something for him or her. But before you step out onto the floor and start actually moving to the music, you need to ask yourself five important questions:

1. Will the party I am dealing with be able to do or deliver what I want?
2. What will it cost me?
3. What will I get?
4. What will I get on condition?
5. What must I do to satisfy the conditions?

For example, in my business, if you want to produce a play off-Broadway in New York City you should:

1. Make certain the party you are dealing with is the author of the play or otherwise owns the play.
2. Know that it will cost you an advance against royalties in the amount of $1,000, more or less, and a royalty of 6% of the gross weekly box-office receipts.
3. Get the rights to produce the play off-Broadway to open within one year of the date of the agreement, and the continuing right to present the play during the continuous run.

4. Conditionally acquire other production rights, such as the right to produce the play in London and on tour, and you will conditionally receive some share of the subsidiary-rights income, that is, from film, television, etc.

5. Get the production rights if the play runs for twenty-one paid performances, and the subsidiary-rights income if the play runs for a certain specified number of performances, graduated between twenty-one and sixty-five performances.

Of course, these terms may vary slightly from play to play, and in a different business the answers will be very different, but the same five conditions should be met.

Once you've got answers and the talking starts, what comes next is not always predictable, definite or easily definable. I wish I could tell you how, precisely, to choreograph your negotiation—which steps to execute in what order—but each negotiation is different; each is an exercise in improvisation. And that's because *people* are involved, each one with different feelings, reactions, passions, prejudices, pride, self-esteem and egos of varying sizes.

Whatever happens, though, however you choose to adapt your moves to the situation in which you find yourself, it's a sure thing you'll need to be quick on your feet and quick with your wit, and that you will exercise all your logic, charm and powers of persuasion as the dance proceeds.

At times during the negotiations you'll feel as if you're tripping yourself up, stumbling through the moves that lead from The Offer to The Deal—The

Acceptance, The Fixing of the Consideration and The Fixing of the Specific Terms (which we'll discuss in the next chapter, "It's a Deal! What's a Deal?"). I know the feeling. Negotiating is not easy. But there are no guarantees that anything worth doing right is going to be easy. And think of the enormous satisfaction you'll feel when the dance is over and you've brought your partner around to exactly the place where you hoped to end up. At this point I want to remind you of something you probably already know: honesty is good business. We in the entertainment industry know who the thieves are. We know whom to trust and whom not to trust. I'm sure it's the same in your field.

I teach a course called "Producing Theater" at the New School for Social Research in New York City. I have taught the course forty-four times. The first time, at the first meeting with the class, I made the point about honesty and said that we knew who the thieves were in the business. I went on to name one or two of them. At the end of the class, a young lady came up to me and said, "I am marrying one of those thieves this weekend." The forty-three times I have taught the course since then, I have said, "We know who the thieves are in the business." Period. End of sentence.

IT'S A DEAL!
WHAT'S A DEAL?

At the end of a successful negotiation, the parties will have made a deal, but in order for that deal to constitute a contract—an agreement that a judge or an arbitrator can enforce, making the parties live up to their obligations—it must contain certain key elements. And it is much easier to prove that these elements exist if they're in writing, which is why I recommend that everyone put the terms of their deal into a written, not just an oral, contract.

I can't tell you the number of people who have said to me, "Oh, I don't need a written contract. He's my best friend and we have an understanding." To which I say, "And every divorce I know was preceded by a romantic courtship and a beautiful wedding." This usually convinces folks that a written contract is a good idea.

A contract can be unilateral or bilateral, and the differences between them are subtle but significant. Although this book is about negotiating a contract, not about analyzing contract law, it's important that you be aware of the differences between these types of contracts, lest you think you have an enforceable agreement when you don't. You'll see what I mean from the examples that follow. Our primary focus, however, will be on bilateral contracts, since they're the kind I recommend my clients use whenever possible.

In a bilateral contract both parties promise to do something ("I promise to buy your car for $2,000 and you promise to sell me your car for $2,000"). In a unilateral contract only one party promises to do something, and the promise is conditional ("I promise to buy your car for $2,000 *if* you deliver the car to my house by nine o'clock tomorrow morning").

Bob Brown, a producer-client of mine, called to say he wanted to sue Mary Smith, the costume designer, for breaching her contract to design and make costumes for the play he was producing. Since he needed the costumes in a hurry, and since he had negotiated with her on a weekend and didn't want to bother me, he had put together his own letter of agreement.

Now I don't mind being consulted on weekends; I very often am. Most of my clients know that I'd rather be "bothered" before they make an agreement than after, when it's fallen apart. In any event, here's Bob's letter:

March 15, 1995

Dear Mary:

I promise to pay you the sum of $6,400 to design and construct thirty-two costumes for my play *Going South*. The costumes will all be constructed of blue denim, ten for men, twenty for women and two for children, in the sizes set forth in the Exhibit A annexed.

The show goes into rehearsal April 15, 1995, and I will need them all completed by then. I will pay you $2,000 upon completion of five costumes, and the balance upon completion of the rest.

Thank you for helping me out at this time.

Sincerely,

/s/

Bob Brown

I had to tell Bob that, although he writes a nice letter and the exhibit annexed clearly set forth the sizes and details of the needed costumes, he couldn't sue Mary. Mary had not breached any contract provision, since it was a unilateral contract and she had not promised to do anything. Only if Mary had in fact designed and constructed the costumes on time would there have been an acceptance of the offer and thus an enforceable agreement between them.

Here is how Bob should have written the letter if he wanted to make sure that he got the costumes on time or had a legal remedy if she defaulted in delivering:

March 15, 1995

Dear Mary:

I promise to pay you the sum of $6,400 to design and build thirty-two costumes for my play *Going South*, and you promise to design and build the costumes in accordance with the specifications set forth in Exhibit A annexed. The costumes will all be constructed of blue denim, ten for men, twenty for women and two for children.

The show goes into rehearsal April 15, 1995, and you agree to complete and deliver all of the costumes by then. I will pay you, and you agree to accept, $2,000 upon completion of five costumes, and the balance upon completion of the rest.

Thank you for helping me out at this time.

Sincerely,   Accepted and Agreed To:

/s/   /s/

Bob Brown   Mary Smith

In this bilateral version of the letter, both parties promise to do something. Bob promises to pay and Mary promises to design and build the costumes. If either party does not live up to their promise, they can be sued and held responsible.

THE FIVE ELEMENTS
OF A CONTRACT

In "Setting the Stage" I mentioned that the negotiating parties had to execute some essential steps in the "dance" of deal-making if their interchange was to result in an enforceable agreement. Now we'll consider the five essential elements of a contract—offer, acceptance, consideration, specific terms and responsible parties—in greater detail.

THE OFFER

An offer, from a legal point of view, is exactly what it sounds like. One party promises (offers) to do, or not do, something if the other party promises to do, or not do, something. It's as simple as that. If either party does not keep the promise, and all of the other contract elements are present, the injured party can have the court make the other party keep the promise or pay the injured party for the damage done by not keeping it.

THE ACCEPTANCE

The acceptance occurs when one party says, "I accept your offer," or uses some other unconditional language which means exactly that. You cannot accept an offer by accepting part of it and rejecting any other part. If a party offers to build an agreed-upon theatrical set for

$25,000 and the other party says, "Okay, you can build my set, but I will only pay you $20,000," that is not an acceptance; it's a counter-offer. If the set builder then says, "No deal, I need $22,500," that's a counter-counter-offer. Not until one party says unequivocally, "Okay, I accept the offer," is there an acceptance.

THE CONSIDERATION

"Consideration," in a legal context, is the inducement to a contract—that which each party promises to give the other party, or promises to do for the other party, or promises to refrain from doing. The amount of the consideration is immaterial; the court doesn't care what it is or what it's worth—only that it exists.

If Alice promises to sell a brand-new Cadillac to Philip for $20, and Philip agrees to pay, there is consideration. In fact $2, $200, $2,000 or $20,000—all or any of these sums would be consideration adequate to meet the contractual requirement.

If, on the other hand, a doting Aunt Mary promises to give a brand-new Cadillac to her nephew Harold just because she loves him, there is no consideration and no contract. Harold hasn't promised to do or not do anything in exchange for the Cadillac, and so if Aunt Mary changes her mind about making the gift, Harold can't do anything about it in a court of law.

THE SPECIFIC TERMS

If the contract is to be legally enforceable, the parties to it must be speaking the same language and have the same understanding of the words being used to spell out what they're agreeing to. Vague or imprecise language must be avoided; the terms of the agreement should be stated clearly and precisely.

For example, a producer agrees to hire a director to direct a play to open on Broadway sometime during the 1995–1996 season. The producer and director do not come to any agreement about the amount to be paid the director, the date on which the play will go into rehearsal, or the size and placement of the director's billing credit. Since these important terms of the hiring transaction have not been specified and agreed upon, there is no contract, merely a tentative arrangement that either party may break at will.

THE RESPONSIBLE PARTIES

As a general rule, the parties to a legally enforceable agreement must be of sound mind and legal age. If a party is drunk, mentally deficient or in other ways incompetent or emotionally impaired, the contract is not enforceable. Keep in mind, however, that there are some laws in each of the states which make minors responsible under certain circumstances.

ORAL AND IMPLIED CONTRACTS

Although the law in most states requires that real estate and a few other transactions be in writing, most agreements need not be written to be enforceable, as long as all of the elements of a contract exist. In fact, it's possible to have a contract without either party having spoken a word, with its terms being implied rather than spoken or written. It happens all the time.

When you get on the bus and put the change in the fare box, neither you nor the bus driver has to say a word. There is an implied contract with all of the elements necessary to have an enforceable agreement. You paid your fare, which is the consideration for the implied promise to give you the bus ride that you accepted by implication. The terms are clearly understood, and it is assumed that you and the bus driver are responsible parties.

The same is true when you plunk down a ten-dollar bill for a ticket to see a movie and the ticket-seller gives you the ticket and change. An enforceable agreement has been established. If you pay and the theater doesn't show you the movie, you have the right to sue and recover the cost of the ticket.

Once you and your negotiating partner come to a meeting of the minds on the terms of your deal, you are wise to put them in writing. Anything from an informal letter to a formal document loaded with details will do. In the entertainment business we often write something called a "deal memo," used in the interim between negotiations and the preparation of full, written documentation. (For an idea of the range of options available, please see the sample documents in the appendixes.)

While in the explanations and examples above I have tried to set forth the principles of contract law that you need to be aware of when conducting negotiations, the body of contract law is very large and can be quite complicated. I will give you the same advice that I give to my clients (all of whom can act, dance, sing or do whatever they do better than I can) when they are on the verge of messing up a contract. "I'll make a deal with you," I say. "I won't act/dance/sing, and you won't do contracts." (For a while I was making the same deal with my author-clients; then I started writing books and I had to change the deal.)

WHO SHOULD DO THE TALKING?

Whether a deal leading to a contract is negotiated by the party who wants something or by someone who speaks on their behalf, it is crucial that the person doing the talking knows what he or she is talking about.

If the subject area in which you will be negotiating is unfamiliar, you have two choices: you can become an instant expert in the field, learning everything you can about the particular item or matter being negotiated. This may mean purchasing books, visiting the library, interviewing experts, taking courses and whatever else is necessary to learn about the subject at hand. Or, you can hire someone who is already an expert in this particular field and let that person do the negotiating for you. (If you're in a new field involving new technology, it's likely that you're the expert and will need to train your negotiator in the concepts and terminology he or she will need in order to negotiate on your behalf. See Ground Rule 8, "Define Your Terms.")

If you're seeking a partner for your professional firm, it might be wise to engage a head-hunter to assist you. If you're looking for a publisher to publish a book you wrote, you'd do well to find a good agent or attorney to represent you. If you're in the entertainment industry, it's helpful to have someone well versed in contract law speaking for you, because, as I said in the previous chapter, it's a complicated subject.

Whatever decision you make about using a representative, to save time and energy and to minimize confusion, I caution my clients against talking to the other party's representative and advise that all communications about the deal go through me. Sometimes, however, there are occasions when it is more practical for my client to conduct negotiations without me—for example, when the other party is not represented by counsel and my presence might therefore seem intimidating. In such a situation, I may suggest that the interested parties talk at least until they have identified all of the relevant issues between them, at which point I can feed my client information on more items to be discussed, or I can get into the act myself. When I do enter the process my role will be to clarify the items they have discussed and agreed upon, identify the items they may have missed or been unable to settle between themselves and prepare the written document containing the agreed-upon terms. The goal is to make the best deal, and if the best deal seems more likely to result from the interested parties doing most of the negotiating, then that's the way to do it.

Regardless of who does the negotiating, it is important to establish that the parties doing it have the authority to speak for the parties they're representing. I must know from my client that when I make a commitment on his or her behalf, the commitment is firm and that later, the rug will not be pulled out from under me. And I want assurance that the same situation exists between my negotiating partner and his or her client; that their commitment is a real commitment. Try not to get stuck negotiating with someone who has no authority to make a commitment. It can be an exercise in futility and is always a frustration. But if ever you are faced with this situation and there is nothing—absolutely, for sure *nothing*—you can do about it, then avoid committing to anything yourself until you have firm confirmation of what the other party will and will not agree to, and the terms are acceptable to you.

Finally, it's important to know when to keep your mouth shut. It isn't always easy, but whatever you say you are pretty much stuck with, so be careful not to offer something that you are not prepared to deliver.

The determination about who should do the talking, who should do the listening, who should keep their mouth shut—and when—will have to be made as circumstances dictate. What you are after are results, and how you achieve them will vary from negotiation to negotiation, sometimes from day to day. If you feel you're getting some mixed messages now as well as further along in this book about whether and how to use an attorney (or other representative) in your negotiations, you're right—you are. But that's okay. There is no definitive answer; there is no fixed rule about when it is best for the principals to talk and when it is best for their representatives to talk, just as there is no single way to accomplish the desired outcome. If the art of negotiation were an exact science, I would be able to give you the formula. Absent a formula, you must use your common sense, good judgment and intuition—key components of all art forms. And negotiation is indeed an art!

ETIQUETTE & ETHICS I

No matter who does the talking, whether it's you or your representative, be aware that what you say before the negotiations start—and how you say it—has an influence on the results you'll achieve.

There's an old legal adage: if the law is on your side, talk about the law; if the facts are on your side, talk about the facts; if neither is on your side, then yell loudly.

Some misguided lawyers I've dealt with seem to think that if they can overpower me at the beginning of a negotiation, they will have gained some advantage. But it doesn't work that way. Loud posturing and an overbearing manner only serve to make me angry.

You can get a lot more from most people with honey than with vinegar—and sometimes some other liquid refreshments can further the discussion. One of the earliest and certainly among the most enjoyable negotiation techniques I learned I call "Negotiation by Scotch." I learned it from Allen Whitehead, an associate of one of the most famous Broadway composers, Frank Loesser. Frank had just formed Music Theatre, Inc., a company in the business of licensing stock and amateur rights in musical plays, and Allen was putting it all together, trying to acquire shows. Both Frank and Allen were charmed and fascinated by *The Fantasticks*, which I represented, and they were anxious to obtain the licensing rights. (I must credit their foresight, since at that time, in 1960, *The Fantasticks* was having great difficulty just staying alive at the Sullivan Street Playhouse, a little theater in Greenwich Village. How did they know that it would become the longest-running show in American history, now in its thirty-sixth year?)

The negotiations were very complicated and it was not advisable to try to work out the details on the telephone. Since their office at 116 West 57th Street in New York City was located between my office and my home, it made sense for me to stop off and see them at the end of the day. Our negotiations extended over a period of months, and I can't say I regretted the time it took.

Whenever I arrived at their office, before settling down to work we would always have a Scotch or two—made even more enjoyable by the fact that they always had my favorite brand on hand and I wasn't drinking alone. Caveat: while the mood of conviviality was a great preliminary to our negotiating sessions, I soon discovered that it was important to keep my wits about me—and the Scotch at arm's length—once the actual negotiations began.

While I recognize that it's somewhat rare for negotiations to proceed in an atmosphere of conviviality, it is absolutely essential that at the very least they occur in an atmosphere of civility. Goon tactics are for hoodlums and may work for extortion or blackmail, but they certainly don't work for good, solid deal-making, nor do less obvious expressions of hostility and rudeness, such as:

- not returning a telephone call;
- not returning several telephone calls;
- making a date to meet and showing up late;
- making a date to meet and not showing up at all;
- not calling to apologize for not showing up;

- showing up for a meeting looking like something the cat dragged in;
- adopting a negative, belligerent tone at the beginning of a discussion or in the course of negotiating;
- compulsively nit-picking and haggling over inconsequential issues;
- interrupting the other party in the presentation of a point or idea, or trying to dispute the other party's point without having heard it fully explained;
- failing to consider a peacemaking compromise proposal even when negotiations have altogether broken down.

Not responding to telephone calls is not only rude, it is also a terrible negotiating tactic. It breeds anger and frustration in the negotiation partner, which is sure to have a negative effect on the course of the bargaining when it eventually resumes.

After suffering repeated episodes of bad behavior from several nonresponsive parties, I came up with a tactic that works well for me. When a series of my phone calls go unanswered, I fax the offending party the following letter:

(Date)

Mr. Peter Anyman   Fax #(212) 987-6543

Dear Peter:

You are bordering on, or maybe you've stepped over, the edge of rudeness.

You were coming to New York, so I arranged for my client to come to the city. You canceled, so I canceled

my client's trip also. My own calendar I also maneu-
vered to accommodate you. Plans change, okay. That
can happen and is understandable.

What I am having trouble understanding is the umpteen
number of telephone calls I have placed to you that
have gone unanswered, with not even a word from a
secretary or associate as to when we will talk, if ever.

I was under the impression that we had some things to
talk about. Maybe I was wrong and we don't. Should I
give up?

Disturbed, almost upset, not yet angry (getting there)
but puzzled —

/s/

Donald C. Farber

What usually happens then is that "Mr. Anyman" calls
me back in about two minutes.

Feel free to copy this letter word for word and fax
it yourself. (If you *really* want to get the other person's
attention and emphasize the need for timeliness, consider sending it by overnight air courier.)

Being reasonable while negotiating is just as important
as being polite. You'd be amazed at some of the crazy
posturing and ridiculous demands that otherwise intelligent folks can exhibit during a negotiation. It's as if
they have a death wish! They back themselves into an
impossible negotiating corner and then, rather than lose
face, they stick to their guns.

If someone believes that he is Napoleon Bonaparte,
it's hard to convince him that he should accept employ-

ment in any job less than emperor. To believe you own a Porsche when the car you're driving around in is a Jeep can mess up your driving; the two vehicles function differently. To believe that you can impose your wishes on someone because you own something you think they would die for, when in fact they are only mildly interested, can foul up your negotiating.

This sort of irrational behavior occurs when parties lose contact with the reality of their bargaining power. They're in the wrong ballpark, they have misplaced their emphasis, forgotten what's most important to them. In subsequent chapters you will learn how to conduct a reality check on bargaining power.

I have discovered in my business that there are really only two ways to accomplish something: I can say "please," and if that doesn't work, I can sue them. (Sure, I could also threaten to sue, but good lawyers don't make idle threats.) Consequently, I say a lot of "pleases." I recommend that you do, too. Yes, I know all about "creative talent" and "poetic license" and "artistic temperament." But these excuses for bad behavior do not impress me, because I know a large number of wonderfully talented individuals who are fairly normal human beings, without any hysteria, outrageous demands or tantrums, who work in and make a living from the business and who manage to control their egos, in spite of their most unusual talent. It's possible. Talent and tantrums are *not* synonymous.

A WORD ABOUT ETHICS

The ethics of negotiation dictate that we all play by the same rules. Just as I avoid talking directly to the other party if they are represented by counsel, if they are not represented I go out of my way to make sure that they get a fair shake. I prepare a contract in which I concede to them all of those things that I think, in fairness, they should have, even if they lacked the knowledge to ask for them. But after I have done this and the party has left my office, written contract in hand, I hope they won't then hire an attorney to start negotiating with me on the agreement in which I have already made all the concessions. That would be unfair and a waste of everyone's time.

THE GROUND RULES

KNOW WHO YOU'RE NEGOTIATING WITH

The more you know about the person you are dealing with, the better you will be able to deal and the more likely you will be to accomplish your objective.

Negotiating is easiest, of course, when you know the people, when it happens among friends, or when you can bring together parties who are already eager to connect, or when you can convince them that they are absolutely essential to one another's success and happiness. We all enjoy playing the matchmaker, whether for a romance or a business deal, and if you have the opportunity to "marry" two of your clients or two of your friends, you're ahead of the game.

What a pleasure it was for me when I could arrange a marriage between my client Kurt Vonnegut and my client Duke Ellington. They were to collaborate on a musical stage adaptation of the film *The Hustler*. And not only was it a dream of a deal to arrange, it was a cinch for me to find a producer when I could offer two such famous personalities working together. Unfortunately, the production never happened, because the Duke died while he was working on the project.

Someone is sure to raise the subject of attorney conflict of interest whenever they hear about a single attorney representing two clients in the same deal. In the entertainment industry, however, this is very often the way things happen. It's only natural for a lawyer to put his author-client together with his producer-client, for instance, because they have a community of interest, not a conflict of interest.

I recently asked a producer-client to go to a reading of a musical play written by another client of mine. He went and became so enamored of the work that he wanted to produce it. There was no conflict of interest on my part; to the contrary. If I had not urged my producer-client to attend the reading, he would never have been exposed to the work and would never have ended up producing it.

If both parties trust the attorney, no problem exists. Even in those instances when there is a potential conflict, my clients almost always have trusted my judgment and insisted that I represent them in the negotiations, even though I would be representing both sides. They knew I would make every effort to prepare agreements both fair and good for both parties to the agreements. It's nice to have that kind of trust. But if either party feels uneasy about my representing both, I insist that that person get other representation.

Any smart negotiator will tell you that if you can arrange for two parties to be dependent upon each other you will be in a better position to convince both of them that they should get together. The late, legendary Hollywood agent Swifty Lazar had a technique to arrange this: he would approach a famous film star and tell her that a very famous producer wanted her for a film and that he, Swifty, would be happy to represent her. Then he would go to a very famous producer and tell him that a famous film star wanted to work for him and that he, Swifty, would be happy to make the deal for him.

He would convince each party that the other wanted him or her and, each being famous but insecure, they'd be flattered by the attention being paid to them. More than flattered, each would end up with a deal that they wanted. In the meantime, Swifty would gain two important new clients.

Obviously, most deals are not negotiated among friends and acquaintances, and your negotiating counterpart will be someone you don't know and may never have heard of. It's up to you to find out everything you can about him or her. If you don't know the person, find someone who does. A few well-placed telephone calls can result in a lot of information.

For instance, if you are a playwright who wants a certain director to produce your play, it would be useful to know that he always casts his wife. If your play just happens to have a starring role for a woman who happens to be about the same age as the director's wife, it will have a far better chance of being produced, since the director would have more than a professional interest in the property and might go out of his way to produce it.

If you represent a stock company in Kansas City or a public school in Minneapolis, and you want to present a copyrighted play, you will have to deal with an agency that controls the license and grants production rights for that play—most likely one of the four most important licensing agencies in New York City. To get the best deal, it would help you to know something about the style of each agency. I deal with all four of them and I can assure you that the person in charge of each is as different from the other three as possible, and I approach each of them differently, using different words and a different style. I might joke and carry on with one of them, while another would think me rude if I behaved in such a fashion. One agent is very informal in his attire, manner and approach to life, while another wouldn't be caught dead outside his home without a necktie and a very conservative suit.

When you make inquiries and learn about the people you're negotiating with, you're sure to hear at some point about the nit-pickers, people who have to find twenty-seven or more things wrong with every proposal, no matter how thoroughly it is researched and presented. And at some point in your career you're sure to deal with people who are insecure and unfamiliar with whatever it is they are negotiating. If offered $5, they'll ask for $6, if offered nine months they'll ask for twelve months, if offered 4% they'll ask for 6%—for no logical reason other than a need to ask for something more than is being offered, even if the original offer is more than fair by any standard. When negotiating with this kind of person, you will structure your offer differently than if you were dealing with a confident, more knowledgeable person.

Sometimes the person you're negotiating with is not the actual decision-maker, and in that case you need to find out about the person who is. If you're dealing with someone who must run to a superior for a response, then it's the superior you must actually be convincing.

Other negotiators are procrastinators; they have trouble making decisions and sometimes, to stall, use the excuse of having to run to someone else for an answer. When this happens, try to minimize the telephone calls, letters, faxes and other kinds of back-and-forth communication by arranging a meeting where all the decision-makers are gathered in one room. If necessary, get on a plane and go to them; it will probably be less expensive than all the delays.

We all react differently to different stimuli. Knowing what someone's reaction to a particular stimulus is likely to be makes it a lot easier to know just how to stimulate that person to agree with what you want.

KNOW THE PEOPLE WHO WORK FOR THE PEOPLE YOU NEGOTIATE WITH

A busy person must return a lot of calls in the course of the day, and the associate who answers the phone is in a position to put one of those messages (yours, you hope) on top, or to remind that person that a certain call (yours) might be important.

Cultivate these people; be as friendly as you can with them. Learn their first names and make a point of communicating with them on a personal level. Be cordial but not intrusive. Get a sense of how busy they are when they answer the phone. If they don't sound pressed for time, they'll probably welcome a short conversation with you. The snow, or lack of it, is always a good subject to chat about until the person you are waiting for gets off the phone—at least that always works for me when I phone someone in Canada. The rain is the subject I talk about when calling England. In New York City the most popular subject is that lousy cross-town traffic; around any holiday, the traffic is worse and even more on people's minds. And you can always fall back on what most people like to be told, which is how efficient they are in managing such a busy job.

Being nice never hurts, and it can help. For example:

After many weeks of trying to get a commitment from a television company to sign a client of mine to produce an adaptation of a general-release film for TV, and being repeatedly put off by the general counsel for the company, I had a discussion with his associate. In the course of our exchange of ideas, I told him the problem I was having with his office. He knew my client's work and was most sympathetic.

That very afternoon, the attorney who had been avoiding my calls for days telephoned to say that he was sitting with his associate and wanted to talk with me about the deal.

I had made a friend in that office and that friend made the deal happen.

I deal with a large number of agents and attorneys who are active people. I assure you that I have quicker access to most of these busy folks because I know their secretaries' names. I ask for his or her name on the initial call and I write it on a Rolodex card under the name of the party I'm negotiating with. (Make sure you get the name right, in case you ever need to address mail to the attention of the secretary. As the inimitable Talullah once said: "I don't care what they say about me as long as they spell my name right.") And make certain that you have the proper title for this person. When the party you are speaking with says to you, "Please, I am her assistant, not a secretary," or "I am his associate," you had best make sure that in the future you address that person by the label he or she prefers.

In addition to giving you quicker access to your negotiating counterpart, his or her assistant (if well disposed toward you) may give you a lot of information that will be helpful to you in the negotiation itself. It's possible, in the course of friendly chatting with the assistant, to learn something about his or her boss' marital status, children, grandchildren, hobbies, vacations, arrival and departure times, likes and dislikes, etc. And it bears repeating that the more you know about the party you are negotiating with, the better you will be able to deal with that party and accomplish your objective.

KNOW THE IDIOSYNCRASIES OF THE INDUSTRY

While it is essential to learn as much as you can about the people you're negotiating with, it also pays to know the particular (sometimes even peculiar) characteristics of the industry you're dealing with and the people who work in it.

The theater business, for example, is a paranoid business (maybe for very good reasons). It is insecure, ego-oriented and time-sensitive—three factors you must always keep in mind when trying to make a theater deal.

Don't these same factors affect most all businesses? you may ask. Well, yes and no, but not to the same extent. In the theater world the insecurities are greater, sometimes unbelievable; the egos are bigger, sometimes inconceivable; and the time demands are intense, sometimes unachievable.

When you go into your first meeting knowing that the people you're dealing with are likely to feel insecure, anxious and distrustful—because that's in the nature of their business—it makes a big difference in how you set the stage, structure the deal and conduct the negotiations. You know what you're up against, but even more important, you know quite a bit about what *they* are up against.

The tremendous insecurity of show business often provokes odd behavior from the people who work in it, behavior that can make or break a deal. Take the story of Zia Mohyeddin, for instance.

Zia Mohyeddin, a Pakistani actor, went to England and washed dishes so that he could study at the Royal Academy. His appearance, in 1961, in a play at Oxford prompted critic Kenneth Tynan to write: "I have seldom been exposed to such intensity of feeling, coupled with such clarity of utterance, speed of delivery and precision of gesture. Physically, Mr. Mohyeddin is no Teuton, but he would have no trouble playing young Mediter-raneans, in whom Shakespeare abounds; there lies my hint, and I hope someone takes it up."

What a splendid tribute from England's most important, most illustrious critic! And someone did "take it up." Zia was offered the role of Romeo at the Old Vic, opposite Dorothy Tutin who would be playing Juliet. Dorothy was then at the top of her career, one of the most beautiful, talented and important serious actresses in England.

The only hitch was that for Zia to appear in *Romeo and Juliet*, he had to do something about the part he had agreed to play in *Lawrence of Arabia*, a film that was going into production simultaneously. When he explained his problem to David Lean, the director of the film, David said he would accommodate Zia by giving him a part earlier in the shooting instead of the more important role he had originally intended to play. So Zia was cast in the part of the trainer who teaches Lawrence (Peter O'Toole) how to ride a camel, and who gets shot at the well early on.

Well, as fate would have it, Zia and Peter Hall, the director of *Romeo and Juliet*, weren't getting on very well. It often happens in the theater that actors and directors have disagreements which, so long as they're kept in control, don't hurt the play; in fact, the creative tension might even help. But after prolonged disagreement with his director, Zia made a mistake. Two days before the opening, he asked Peter Hall if he should quit. To his shock, Peter Hall said yes, and the play opened with Brian Murray as Romeo. On opening night in London, Zia was alone in Italy. The part Zia gave up in Lawrence went to an unknown chap by the name of Omar Sharif.

Lest you think only a young, relative newcomer can fall vulnerable to the insecurity of show business, let me mention that my friend Joan Bennett, the movie star, made seventy-four movies before her then-husband shot her then-agent in a fit of romantic jealousy. After that Joan never made another movie.

When all is said and done, we behave like the conditioned creatures we are. Every action has a reaction, but we all react differently to various stimuli. Knowing what someone's reaction will be to a particular stimulus can help us adjust our actions to stimulate that person's willingness to agree with what we want. In negotiation, that knowledge is power.

GROUND **2** RULE

ANALYZE YOUR SITUATION

Once you have a feeling for the individuals with whom you'll be negotiating and the industry in which they move, it is time to zero in on the particular deal you are about to negotiate. If you lay the groundwork well now—analyzing your situation and developing a game plan—you'll increase your bargaining power later.

Here's how I laid the groundwork when I had to convince the parties (which included unions, landlords and owners of certain dramatic works) who dealt with a not-for-profit theater I represented, that my client should be treated differently from other not-for-profit theaters. First I gave them the following background:

There are hundreds of not-for-profit theaters throughout the United States, all vying for grants from corporate America and the National Endowment for the Arts. Box-office receipts are almost never enough to cover the expenses of production and the running expenses. Many of the theaters are in small communities with a limited theater-going population, and the plays cannot run long enough to recover the pre-production and production expenses necessary to mount them. Even in the larger communities, the audience ready to patronize serious dramatic theater (often experimental), which is the output of most of these organizations, is very limited to begin with and the competition keen. And as not-for-profit theaters, they cannot entice investors with an eye to making a profit, so they must rely on grants which are in the nature of gifts.

In light of this background, I put forward the following reasons for giving "my" theater preferential treatment:

1. It provides the community with a much-needed cultural service.
2. It attracts patrons from all over the country and other parts of the world, bringing not only prestige but business and wealth to the community.
3. It is not competing with the local profit-making establishments and deserves support.
4. It has the confidence of the federal government, which has granted it $500,000 in 1995 alone.
5. It often operates at a large deficit and needs help.
6. Its creative personnel are all willing to work for less than they would earn in another environment.
7. Its work is unique, and no other comparable theater company produces work of such high quality.
8. Everyone else dealing with it has given it preferential treatment.

Be prepared for the other party to say, "Well, isn't that the case with *every* not-for-profit theater?" Your answer has to be a resounding "no!" You have to establish that your company is really different, really unique, and that's why famous stars and superstars have been willing to work there for practically nothing.

Here's how I developed my strategy in another, quite different, situation. A client of mine conceived of a musical revue that would feature the music of a very popular theater composer. The ultimate goal was to bring the revue to Broadway or off-Broadway in New York City. The conceiver was an unknown director who had little or no chance of getting the rights to present the revue in New York at that time. The estate of the deceased composer was willing to grant us the rights to present the revue in San Francisco, but after San Francisco we were required to negotiate for the rights on a city-by-city basis—Chicago, then Miami, then Austin, Texas—a tedious business. Finally, in Austin, something happened that we'd been waiting for: unanimous raves in the newspaper reviews.

I called the attorney for the composer's estate and, before he could say a word, I mentioned the rave reviews in Texas. I outlined for him the following reasons for granting the rights for a New York production:

1. Every production so far had received good reviews and the latest production, in Austin, brought all raves.
2. Since all the music in the revue comes from the composer's musical plays, additional stage productions of the revue would generate interest in those plays, possibly encouraging other producers to try and acquire stage rights to them, thus creating additional income for the estate of the deceased composer.
3. The revue might also create additional interest in the original-cast albums of the composer's musical plays, thus providing the estate with additional revenue.
4. The young director, although without a New York credit, had directed many musical plays outside New York City, all of which had been received enthusiastically by the local critics.

5. The director had done his homework and already made preliminary arrangements to finance the move to New York. In fact he was prepared right there to write a check for a non-returnable advance against royalties for the option to produce the play in New York City.

6. There was a 199-seat theater available immediately, and a good deal could be made on that house. The timing was perfect.

Notice that in both of these situations I analyzed how my clients' situations differed from the usual, thus presenting the other side with a number of reasons for giving my clients preferential treatment. In doing so, I demonstrated respect for the other side as well as for my client, which helped establish an atmosphere of trust in which we could work toward a mutually satisfactory deal.

You can do the same thing with your negotiations. Just sit down before you start, analyze your situation and make a list of what is special about it. You'll be surprised at how much you come up with.

GROUND **3** RULE

ASSESS YOUR
BARGAINING POWER

When you start betting in a poker game, it's a good idea to count your chips and look carefully at your cards. When you go into a negotiating session, it's a good idea to estimate your bargaining power—and that of the other party—before you do much talking.

Nothing exposes a negotiator's inexperience more glaringly than making an exorbitant demand or offering a ridiculously low price. If your demand is excessive, the other party will not bid against it and you'll be out of the game before you start. If your offer is too stingy, no one will want to make a counteroffer and again you're out of the game. For example:

- A never-published author discovers a small publisher who is willing to publish his book. He asks the publisher for an advance against royalties of $100,000. He's out of the game; almost never will a publisher risk so much on an unknown writer. The figure demanded should be around $20,000, which might result in the author's getting a $10,000 or $15,000 advance.

- A film producer comes to me to option the film rights to a successful short story by one of my well-known author clients. He offers $1,000. He's out of the game; nothing less than about $10,000 makes sense, and I'll not even make a counteroffer since I'll not have confidence that a producer so ill-informed could ever attract the people and capital to make the film.

Put simply, bargaining power is the extent to which you can influence the other party because of the strength of your position or the weakness of his or hers. Here are some points to consider:

THE STATURE OF THE PERSON OR PROPERTY BEING SOUGHT (AND OF THE PERSON DOING THE SEEKING)

In film negotiations, Tom Cruise has more bargaining power than a novice actor. The composer of four Broadway musicals has greater negotiating clout than a never-produced composer. An author who has had eight books on the best-seller list is in a much stronger position than an unpublished writer.

When the representative of a negotiating party has an identifiable name and is an acknowledged expert in the field being negotiated, it also doesn't hurt. Not infrequently I hear, "Oh, you're the guy who wrote all those books and edits the entertainment industry contracts volumes," and there's a great upsurge in my bargaining power.

THE VALUE OF THE ITEM AROUND WHICH THE NEGOTIATIONS ARE CENTERED

How badly does the other party want the item? After all, something is worth whatever anyone is willing to pay for it. Collectors are always willing to pay extra for the item that would round out their collection, whether it be stamps or coins or cups and saucers.

If the negotiations center around a literary property— a book or a play—what has been the reaction to it from experienced professionals in the field of publishing and theater? And how time-sensitive is the item? An interest in the manufacture and sale of hula hoops at the peak of the fad was far more valuable than it is now.

THE AMOUNT OF EXCITEMENT GENERATED BY THE PROPERTY

Is the property "hot"? Are there other potential buyers? If you are a never-produced playwright in the boondocks and four New York-based producers are trying to option your play, you can assume you have strong bargaining power. And this happens in the theater business. Some not-for-profit theater somewhere will produce a play that causes a buzz in the theater community. Professional producers will rush to wherever to see it and, if they like it, try and negotiate the rights to move it to Broadway or off-Broadway. (If, on the other hand, as usually happens, a play opens in a regional or other not-for-profit theater without making a splash, the playwright would be wise to know that his bargaining power in relation to a move to a commercial venue is next to nil.)

THE AMOUNT OF MONEY, TIME AND ENERGY ALREADY TIED UP IN THE PROPERTY

Your bargaining power is increased when the other party has a vested interest in the continuation of the project. To the extent that you're aware of the amount and nature of that vested interest, you might be able to improve your own position without damaging the other side's—an important consideration when you want to sow good will toward a future working relationship.

For example, in my business we deal all the time with something called "options." A party may agree to pay an author $20,000 for a one-year option on the rights to make a film based on a particular novel, and another $20,000 for a one-year extension of the option. Now the two years have passed and the potential film producer has spent $40,000 on the options and maybe $100,000 to have a screenplay written, but has not yet been able to sign a director or arrange for the financing of the film.

The producer approaches the author's representative to extend the option for still another year, and this time offers a fee of $30,000. Even though all of the option payments may be considered payments against the purchase price of the film rights (in this case $300,000), the producer has already invested a lot of money, time and energy, all of which will go down the drain unless he can renew the option.

At this point the author's representative has a lot of bargaining power, but he must remember to exercise caution. While he's now in an ideal position to obtain maximum benefit for his client, he must do so without imposing conditions or demanding concessions that may make it impossible for the producer to make the film.

There are several things he could ask for that would benefit his client without hurting the producer. For one, the cost of the film rights to the novel (set at $300,000 two years ago) should increase, since the cost of making the film will have increased dramatically during the time of the options. What was a $20,000,000 film budget two years ago might become a $30,000,000 budget in the end. The author's representative could ask the producer to pay the author an extra $50,000 at the commencement of principal photography, which might seem a negligible amount to a producer with a $30,000,000 budget.

For another, the author's representative could ask for some kind of deferred payment, payable to the author only after the investors have recouped their investment. If the film is successful and the investors get their money back, this request should cause minimum pain. The author may also be offered a payment as script consultant and/or production consultant—again a relatively painless offer, since the payment won't be made until the budget has been raised.

By now it has become obvious to you that, at the beginning, with so many variables affecting your bargaining power, and with the potential for those variables to change during the negotiations, it isn't easy to gauge the strength of your position relative to the other party's. But awareness of the *concept* of bargaining power is helpful to your negotiations even when it's difficult to measure that power precisely. If you keep the concept in mind, you'll be on the lookout for patterns and factors that hint at how you stand in relation to your opponent, and your position will become clearer as the negotiations evolve and there's an exchange of ideas.

Negotiating is kind of like a chess game. When the game begins, neither player knows very much about the other player's strengths and weaknesses, but the longer the game goes on, the more you learn about your own strengths as well as your opponent's. Eventually there's a stalemate—neither party wins—or a checkmate, and one party is the victor. The desired outcome in the game of negotiations is different, however: here we want both players to win.

GROUND **4** RULE

THINK CONSTRUCTIVELY

I was going to call Rule 4 "Think Positively," but that doesn't really tell you enough. Positive thinking is fine, but you need more than "positive." You have to think *constructively.*

Positive thinking assumes that agreement will be reached on an item being negotiated. Constructive thinking is the process that makes it happen.

Thinking constructively means placing yourself in the position of the other party and asking yourself the following questions: "How does the other party view this particular item? How would I react if I were asked to give in on this issue?" When you have the answers, you're ready for constructive thinking to take over.

I recently negotiated a contract for a client who was very insecure; he changed his mind as often as his necktie. I would have lengthy discussions with the attorney for the other party and we'd reach some sort of agreement, only to have my client pick it apart—find fault with a concept or criticize the wording. But I knew my client, I knew he wanted to make the deal and that eventually he would sign the agreement, whether happily or unhappily.

The other attorney was getting very testy. He pointed out (none too politely) that we were now discussing a sixth draft. He acted as if it were all my fault, as if he and his client didn't share any blame at all for drafting an agreement that included vague language even after six revisions.

I don't like lecturing another lawyer, but I don't like being verbally abused, either. So I explained to the other attorney in simple language that if he stopped being snotty, I could assure him that the agreement would be signed whether or not he made any further changes. Then I explained that by giving my client a seventh draft in which he clarified the remaining vague language, the attorney could make my client happier without in any way compromising his own client's position. And since our clients were going to be doing a lot of business together over a long term, didn't it make sense to try and please my client (who was going to sign anyway) when it took nothing away from his client's position?

He made the changes. The contract was signed. The deal was closed and all of the parties were happy.

A variation on this negotiating technique of asking someone to give you something that's good for you and involves no sacrifice to them, is to ask him or her to give you something that is good for you but also good for them, even though they may not realize it. And to convince them that what you're asking for is in their interest, also, it is sometimes useful to blame somebody else for the position you take.

For example, if you are a Broadway producer who wants to option a popular novel for adaptation for a big Broadway musical, you will set about acquiring the rights from the novelist and then convey them to the team of book writer, composer and lyricist that you have engaged to prepare the stage adaptation. That team will work on the adaptation for a year or more, receiving advance payments that only rarely compensate them for the amount of work involved; what they count on to really pay them for all their work—they hope—are the royalties from the Broadway production. But more than that, if the stage version is successful, they want to be in a position to sell the motion picture, television and other subsidiary rights.

These rights are so important that any book writer, composer and lyricist of any merit will insist on having them. Therefore, when you as producer bargain with the novelist for the rights to do an adaptation for the stage, you will also bargain for the rights to do a motion-picture adaptation, so that you can convey those rights to the team doing the musical adaptation.

If the novelist refuses to grant film and other subsidiary rights, it's time to think constructively and blame somebody else: simply inform the novelist that if he or she insists on retaining these rights, then forget about getting Stephen Sondheim (*Sweeney Todd; Company; A Little Night Music; Follies; Sunday in the Park with George; Passion,* etc.) or Kander and Ebb (*Cabaret; Kiss of the Spider Woman,* etc.) or Jerry Herman (*Hello, Dolly; Mame,* etc.) to do the music and lyrics, because these artists will absolutely refuse to work on any property for which they cannot sell the film rights.

Faced with the possibility of unheard-of people doing the adaptation (if even unknowns could be found to do it under such circumstances), the novelist is likely to concede the film rights.

And while you're blaming the book writer, composer and lyricist for refusing to work without these rights, you might as well blame the investors, too, for if a successful Broadway play cannot be sold for a movie or a television production, they will not share in the subsidiary-rights income that they have learned to expect from such an investment, and they will not invest in the play. The novelist can certainly understand how the investors' demands make this demand of yours both necessary and feasible.

If the author of a play insists that his or her name be the largest on the program, blame the director. Simply say, "Okay, you just lost Hal Prince, Mike Nichols or Gene Saks as director." The author will be quick to agree that the director's name ought to appear as big or bigger.

And if you are working on a deal that involves more than one party, what you agree upon with the first party will affect other parties who may or may not become involved with the project later. The first party needs to understand that while the two of you have a "common interest," he or she must be prepared "for the sake of the deal" to make the concessions you need to entice other parties to become involved.

"It's all his fault; I had nothing to do with it," is what the technique of blaming somebody else can allow you to do—and in all honesty. It's a very comfortable feeling to be able to give a good reason for getting someone to do something that you want for reasons other than that it's just because you want it. It's an easy victory when you can ask the other party for something that is obviously good for them. Good for you, too, yes, but especially good for them.

GROUND **5** RULE

KNOW WHAT'S IMPORTANT

Since it is rare to get everything you want in a contract, exactly as you want it, negotiating involves the art of compromise. In fact, the very essence of negotiation is compromise—giving up something in order to get something else of at least equal value.

The smart way to compromise is to know how much each element of a contract is worth to you. After you've identified the most important elements—the ones worth fighting for—conceding on the lesser elements is like giving away ice in the wintertime.

For example, I prepared a contract for the acquisition of the rights to produce a stage play. The agent representing the author sent me a five-page, single-spaced letter demanding twenty-one changes in the contract. I carefully decided she could have seventeen of those changes, but not the other four, which were the only ones worth fighting about.

She was thrilled to tell her client that she got seventeen of the twenty-one requested changes. I was happy to tell my client that the concessions we made were not in the least bit important to the substance of the transaction and that we had successfully resisted all of the agent's significant requests.

To anybody in the theater business, there is one element that is always worth fighting about: the billing credit. Fierce battles are waged over whose name comes first and whose name is displayed more prominently in the print ads, the program book and the marquee. This is not totally fatuous (the theater business is, after all, an ego business), as there is often a relationship between the billing credit and the rate of pay. That is, the person whose name is in big and bold type gets more money than the one whose name is in small type.

When a book writer, composer and lyricist work on a play together and all three happen to be of equal stature, there's no fight; each name appears in the usual order—book writer, then composer, then lyricist—with each name having the same size, boldness and prominence of type. (With a list of actors, alphabetical order is often used.) But when one of the parties is better established and better known than the others, the usual hassles about who gets what and who controls what are out on the table. In negotiation the more established party might be persuaded to give up the bigger billing credit (and bigger share of the pie) in exchange for more control over future uses of the property in all media, or for some other consideration.

One of the most famous billing-credit predicaments occurred when Mary Martin and Ethel Merman went on tour together. What a dilemma! Here were two superstars in the same play, two women of equal stature. How to print their names? A side-by-side arrangement in alphabetical order wouldn't do, since we read from left to right and therefore pay more attention to the name on the left. The name on the right *could* be printed in slightly larger type—but clearly, no simple remedy of spacing or type size was going to resolve this situation.

And then some brilliant person came up with the perfect solution: an upside-down program book. The complete contents of the program would be printed twice, with identical copy except for the names of the stars. Depending on which way you picked up your program, either Mary Martin or Ethel Merman might have top billing. When you read to the middle of the book and flipped it, the other star's name was on top all the way through to the end of the program. Talk about an ingenious way of solving an impossible problem!

As important as it is to evaluate the relative significance of each item in a contract before beginning negotiations, it is also important not to concede any item prematurely. In a complicated deal, it is absolutely crucial to know all of the disputed issues before you commit to or concede any one of them; some may be deal-breakers, others, less of a problem (see Ground Rule 6, "Deal with the Deal-Breakers"). In the example below, you will see that before going into the contract negotiation, I developed a list of questions, the answers to which determined the course of action recommended.

My client, a Broadway producer, was in the process of engaging a famous movie star for a new production on Broadway. He wanted the star to stay in the production for a minimum of six months, a customary expectation in the industry; she would commit to three months only. Before we could agree to this reduced time commitment, we needed to know the following:

1. How much did the star expect to be paid?
2. Would the star extend her time commitment if the salary was increased?
3. If the star would extend, for how many months and how much more salary?
4. What would the star be willing to do to help with the publicity for the play?

5. Would the star commit a specific minimum number of hours to publicizing the play at no additional fee?
6. Would the star devote extra time to assisting her replacement, both in acting in the play and in the publicity about the replacement?
7. What expensive extras would the star expect, such as limousine service to and from the theater, and maybe other times as well; remodeling of the dressing room; appurtenances in the dressing room such as television, extra private phones, etc.; living and travel expenses?

Only when we had the answers to all of these questions and to others that would develop from the star's answers, would we be in a position to respond to the contract as a whole.

You must do the same thing. As you and your negotiating partner go through a contract discussing each disputed item point by point, resist all requests to answer yes or no on specific items. Make it clear that you want a mutual exchange of points of view, and that you can only answer after you've heard and discussed *all* the disputed items.

We're all familiar with the story of the four blind men who were asked to describe an elephant. The one who felt the tail said that an elephant is like a piece of rope. The one who felt the elephant's leg said, "No, no, an elephant is like a tree." The one who felt the tusk said, "It's like a sword." And the last one felt the trunk and said that it was like a snake. If you address one part of a complicated agreement without seeing the whole elephant, you are negotiating blind.

GROUND **6** RULE

DEAL WITH THE
DEAL-BREAKERS

When somebody says, "That's a deal-breaker," he or she is usually referring to a contract provision so important that if not granted, the deal is off; or a provision that the other party wants in the contract that he or she simply can't live with. Deal-breakers are serious business. They can cause people to walk away from the negotiations.

As you analyze your situation and figure out your contract priorities before and during the early stages of a negotiation, you will determine what your own deal-breakers are. Sometimes they are unavoidable, although you'll want to keep their number to a minimum. Remember: flexibility and a willingness to compromise are the essence of negotiating and deal-making.

Here's an example of how a deal-breaking situation might be avoided: If you, as the producer of a Broadway play, want to limit the authority of the director with respect to casting, you will likely be faced with a deal-breaker. No self-respecting director would agree to such a contract provision; directors are accustomed to participating in cast selection and having ultimate approval.

Wanting more than the customary say in selecting the cast, you, the wise producer, need to find a way to achieve your goal without creating a contract crisis. You might talk to the director up front about your casting ideas, and get a feel for whether or not the director and you have compatible visions. Or you might make a list of actors you think suitable for the cast, submit it to the director during negotiation and get the director's approval in writing before the director is engaged.

You—still as producer—will also have to take into account the playwright's customary authority in relation to casting, but here you will have a little more leeway. You might accept the playwright's list of approved actors but append a clause reading, "or any other actor of equal stature," giving yourself the right to select someone thought to be of equivalent ability.

In any hiring situation, the parties are likely to have had general discussions about what the work entails and what each other's approach and philosophy are with regard to it. The difficulties—and the potential deal-breakers—arise from what gets left out of these discussions, the specifics that can sometimes be as important as the general provisions. You may, for example, engage an employee and then inform her that the job will require her to travel. When she discovers that this traveling involves being on the road fifty weeks a year, you could have a very unhappy employee on your hands. Had you specified the travel time in the hiring agreement, this item surely would have been a deal-breaker.

Timing can mean everything. Deciding just when to make clear to the other party that an item is a deal-breaker is part of the art of deal-making.

If you commence discussions and it appears early on that you and the other party are not in the same ballpark, it might be wise at that time to make clear how important your deal-breaker items are. By doing so, you will save everyone a lot of time and trouble, bringing to a quick end negotiations that are unlikely ever to result in a comfortable deal.

If, on the other hand, you find you're dealing with someone who is flexible, it might be wise to delay your insistence on the importance of your deal-breaker items until you both have an investment of time in the discussions. By then, the other party will have seen that you are willing to make concessions on many other items even if you must stand fast on the items you consider to be deal-breakers. If your concessions are important enough to the other party, at that stage he or she may be willing to concede what's important to you.

For example: you are engaging a director to direct an off-Broadway production, but if the play enjoys a degree of commercial success, you will want to move it to a Broadway theater. The director you are engaging will, of course, want written into the contract that he has the right to direct the play on Broadway or any other commercial production it may have. This may be a deal-breaker for you, however. If you as producer need a co-producer to help finance the Broadway move, your co-producer may make it part of the deal that you engage a famous director such as Hal Prince or Jerry Zaks. Or you may, on your own, decide that another director would make it easier to sell the play to investors or would be a better choice creatively.

You have a dilemma: you either risk losing the director you want to direct the off-Broadway play, or give up the future possibility of moving the play to Broadway. If you put this item aside for the moment and negotiate all of the other contentious items in the contract to both parties' satisfaction, you can then approach this problem knowing that both of you are trying hard to make a deal in an atmosphere of trust. You can then work out a compromise; for example: you will state in the contract that you will make your best efforts to see that the off-Broadway director is hired for the Broadway production, and if not hired he or she will be paid a satisfactory amount to heal the wound created by the loss of the better job. As the famous stand-up comedian Joe E. Lewis used to say, "What good is happiness? It can't buy money."

The example above illustrates the importance of creating and maintaining a good negotiating atmosphere. Absent such an environment, deal-breakers that are less tangible than specific contract items might proliferate. For example, one of the parties might learn something about the other party that creates distrust. One of the parties might act rudely or behave offensively (not returning phone calls or showing up late for meetings). One of the parties might use vague and confusing language as if deliberately wanting to obfuscate the issues. The party preparing the written agreement might submit a document that does not accurately reflect what was agreed upon in the negotiations. Or one party might call off the deal because a better offer has come along—bad behavior (see "Etiquette & Ethics II"), but it does happen.

Experience will dictate when you must stand on principle and when you can bend. But in arriving at a decision about what is important enough to break your deal, use some discretion. Remember: if you are as stubborn as a jackass, you may end up eating hay.

GROUND 7 RULE

DON'T MAKE THE CONTRACT SO GOOD THAT IT'S BAD

Although it happens too often, I have yet to figure out why a producer may think that he can make a contract with a star that takes unfair advantage of the star. The producer may be rejoicing over the fact that he resisted giving the star the limousine she wanted, having arranged to give her cab money instead, and saved even more money by putting her up in a less than exclusive hotel. If the star is unhappy with the contract, which the producer thinks is a good contract, the star can show up late, sing off-key and report in sick three times a week. Such a contract would be so good for the producer that it is bad for the producer.

If a contract isn't good for both parties, it isn't good for either one. Examples in the entertainment industry abound:

- An ill-advised agent insists on a royalty of 10% of the gross weekly box-office receipts for a playwright-client. That's a good royalty (about 4% higher than usual) resulting in a lousy contract, since informed investors are not likely to invest in a production in which they probably won't see any profit, and so the play is unlikely to be produced.

- The agent for a novelist whose book is to be adapted for a stage play insists on controlling the film rights in the play. That sounds like a good deal for the novelist, but since no first-rate adaptor will adapt a novel for the stage unless he or she controls the future uses of the play, this is a contract that is so good it's bad.

- A producer hires a busy and popular general manager to manage his show, convincing her to take the job for considerably less money than she is accustomed to being paid. What sounds like a deal advantageous to the producer is really a dud. The manager's other well-paying clients will get her attention when they need it, distracting her from the cheapskate producer's show.

- A producer enters into a contract with a set designer who agrees to pay any costs that exceed the amount budgeted for sets—an amount the producer knows is really too little for the job. The set designer will come in on budget with a lousy set that is poorly constructed. The contract is so good, it's bad.

When you try to get something for nothing, you usually end up with nothing. The person supplying the services is going to be dissatisfied with the arrangement and the services supplied are likely to be inferior, delayed or not forthcoming at all. It's not fun to have to refund money to theater patrons when the star they paid to see is "too ill" to perform—and it's a situation that can be avoided.

It's easier—and less costly in the end—to play fair and be reasonable. Put yourself in the position of the other party and ask yourself how you would view this particular item in the contract, how you would react if you were asked to give in on this issue. Then think back to your childhood days, when you hopped onto the see-saw and some scrawny little kid half your weight got on the other end. You came crashing down in a great hurry.

If some fatso got on the other end, he came crashing down and you went sailing. The only way the seesaw was any fun for either of you was when the weight on both sides was fairly well balanced. That's how it is with contracts, too. If you don't deal properly and you put too much weight on your end, you're going to come crashing down and the other party will go sailing.

GROUND **8** RULE

DEFINE YOUR TERMS

As we learned in "It's a Deal! What's a Deal?" negotiated agreements, by definition, must include specific terms if they are to be legally enforceable contracts. It follows that the parties to the agreement will have a similar understanding of what those terms actually mean.

If only that were true! You'd be surprised at how muddled the understanding can become between the time you and the other party reach agreement and the time you see the written document the other party has prepared to formalize it.

Often the culprit is language—wording that is vague or different from what was used in the negotiating sessions. Occasionally the lawyers are to blame. Although lawyers don't have a monopoly on confusing language, they do sometimes use language to confuse. If the language is vague enough, they figure, perhaps they can offer different interpretations that will accrue to their client's benefit should there ever be a dispute about the issue at hand.

Drafting agreements can be a fine art. I antagonize many of my lawyer-colleagues because I insist on keeping the language simple, so that laypeople as well as lawyers can understand it. There are enough words in the English language, I insist, to accurately express an agreement without resorting to highfalutin' legal mumbo jumbo.

Some lawyers, especially those not sure of what they are doing, will talk (and write) in a language that is truly alien and alienating. If it's possible to say something simply with one word, they'll find three words. Instead of the word "grant," the fancy-talker will say "give, devise and bequeath," or "convey, transfer and assign."

If someone pulls this on you, make him or her explain the language being used. Don't be intimidated by long legal-sounding words. If you're on the phone with the person you're negotiating with and he or she says something you don't understand, make sure that you get a simple explanation. If the telephone conversation is unintelligible, you can imagine what sort of written agreement this person will produce. (You would do well to draft it yourself when the time comes; see Ground Rule 10, "Prepare the Document.")

Words have specific meanings that vary from industry to industry, context to context, and we must be sure that all parties to the agreement understand the terms or concepts in the context of the negotiations. The entertainment industry, for instance, is a "percentage" business, and that term gets bandied about a lot. So do expressions such as "gross profits," "net profits," "gross receipts," "net receipts," "deferred gross profits," "deferred net receipts," etc. Since many people in show business share in percentages of the "gross weekly box-office receipts" and in the "net profits" of the producing company, it is crucial that everyone dealing in this context understand the dramatic difference between the two.

Not long ago a clever Broadway producer offered his investors 70% of the net profits of the production company putting on a musical play, keeping only 30% for himself. Since the producer and investors usually share the net profits on a 50/50 basis, on the surface this appeared to be a most attractive offer.

However, if you carefully read the offering literature for this play, you would have discovered that the "generous" producer offering 70% of the net profits was taking a producer's fee of 4% of the gross weekly box-office receipts, going up to 5% after recoupment of all of the production costs—when the usual producer's fee is only 1-2%!

With a successful musical grossing $600,000 a week in box-office receipts, this producer's fee at 4% would be $24,000 a week instead of the customary 1% or $6,000 a week. And who knows when—if ever—the costs of production would be recouped and the producer would have net profits to share with investors at the rate of 50%, let alone 70%? He was giving away pie in the sky in exchange for real cash.

In the film business, too, the term "net profits" is used (even though most people agree with the character in David Mamet's play, *Glengarry Glen Ross*, who shouts, "There *are* no net profits!"), but each film studio has a different definition of the term. One studio's definition is thirty-seven pages long, single-spaced, yet many hours are still required to hash out certain parts of the contract to the satisfaction of all parties.

Despite the difficulty and tedium involved in defining your terms, it's better to do it in negotiations than to have a judge do it later on. And sometimes there are shortcuts. In certain businesses a term is so well established that accountants who work in that industry will come up with definitions acceptable to most people, in which case you insert a clause in your contract that gives you the stated percentage of the item under discussion "as that term is commonly used in the business and as understood by the accounting firm of Blankety-Blank, accountants for the production."

If a percentage payment is to figure anywhere in your contract, be sure the contract also includes a clause giving the party who is to receive the percentage the right to examine the books and records of the other party a reasonable number of times a year at reasonable business hours. (Once a year during regular business hours is what I usually ask for, but this may vary with the type of business and the frequency of the accountings.)

Very often in a film deal when a production company wants to buy the rights to make a film based on a novel, the producer may offer the novelist a percentage of the net profits in exchange for a smaller up-front payment. The producer knows that if and when there are net profits, it will be less painful to make the additional payment to the novelist; after all, by that time all the producer's costs will have been recouped.

When I negotiate a film contract and the producer wants my client to part with the rights to a novel (traditionally, for the life of the copyright) and part of the deal is a share of the net profits, I always argue that the net profits offered are, in reality, part of the purchase price. Then, if the novelist does not receive, by some fixed date, sufficient net profits from the film to cover the full purchase price, the rights to the novel are to revert to the novelist so that they can be sold again.

In other words, if you don't pay the full price, you don't get the whole ball of wax; if you ask the novelist to speculate and the speculative part of the purchase price turns out to be worthless, then you owe the novelist something. Sometimes this argument works and sometimes it doesn't, but it sure is worth a try when someone is telling you how valuable the percentage they are offering is or will be.

In case this discussion makes you look unfavorably upon net profits as a means of payment, it is important to balance the picture and mention that this percentage-payment business can be a superb way of sweetening a deal, making it more attractive to a party. It offers a way to structure compensation by rewarding people for success, or deferring payment until a later, more convenient date.

On a personal note: Since in addition to my legal work on *The Fantasticks* I had done a lot of work of a non-legal nature—helping to raise the budget and otherwise participating in the production work—I ended up with a small percentage of the net profits of the show. During the show's thirty-six-year run, that little percentage has meant a relatively large sum of money to me, proving my maxim: It's what you get a piece of, not how big the piece is, that matters—2% of something is something and 90% of nothing is nothing.

GROUND **9** RULE

KNOW WHEN TO USE PRECEDENTS, WHEN TO BREAK WITH TRADITION AND WHEN TO SAY YOU DON'T KNOW

Trade practices within a particular business or industry usually develop logically, based on common sense and long experience. It makes sense to do something in a certain way, so people do it that way, over and over again. Ultimately a body of precedent is established.

Time passes, situations change, and some precedents outlive their usefulness. We adapt them when possible, break with them when necessary, and begin the process of establishing new precedent all over again.

When new technologies catch us off guard and there is little or no precedent to serve as a guide, we can't stand still but must acknowledge our inadequacy and move ahead as creatively and responsibly as possible.

WHEN TO USE PRECEDENT

Most industries have a body of precedent to start you off on negotiating a deal. Take advantage of it! It will save you a lot of time and aggravation. If you're lucky there will even be prenegotiated contracts—that is, agreements that have been reached with the relevant unions, guilds and trade associations—which you can adopt in their entirety. Just get a copy of the appropriate form, sign on the dotted line, and get on with your business.

If you wanted to produce a play on Broadway, for instance, you would have access to (and sometimes be legally bound to use) thirteen prenegotiated contracts, each of which has been developed between the pertinent union and the League of American Theatres and Producers. These contracts provide minimum provisions for engaging all of the cast and crew needed to produce a play, and will be used "as is" most of the time. If a famous star or a prestigious designer is to be engaged, however, negotiations will result in additional terms that will end up in a rider attached to the standard agreement.

Even if you don't have access to prenegotiated contracts, most likely your field of business has something called "standard industry practice"—a concept that covers a lot of useful ground, even if it sometimes leaves a few bare patches that need further negotiation. (The last time someone asked me to show them a standard theater license agreement, for example, I pulled out *six* "standard" agreements from my files.)

Some standard industry practices are almost never deviated from. In the theater business, for instance, no one may change a word of a script without the playwright's permission; that is standard industry practice. However, if a producer acquires the rights to adapt a novel for the stage (or for a film), the adaptor can do almost anything with the novel—change it, add to it, delete from it—without the novelist having any say whatsoever; that, too, is standard industry practice.

There is one deviation from this practice, but it's an exception that proves the rule, having itself become standard industry practice. The author of an autobiographical novel may wish to grant the rights to an adaptation for stage or film, but only on the condition that the adaptor not depict him or her in an unfavorable light. In this case, the full license customarily enjoyed by the adaptor of a novel for stage or screen becomes somewhat more restrictive.

While sometimes you would be foolish to waste time reinventing the wheel and renegotiating what has already been established as precedent or become standard industry practice, there are times when you and your negotiating counterpart will determine that the standard doesn't accommodate your needs, and that alterations, additions and deletions to the standard agreements must be made.

I lived through such an adventure in the late 1950s and early 1960s when the off-Broadway scene was a fledgling development, just beginning to outgrow its reputation among theatergoers as a bunch of performers amusing themselves in someone's basement. Until then, for fifty years, Broadway was "where it was at."

As I mentioned earlier, I participated in helping to produce *The Fantasticks*. At the time I negotiated the deals necessary to get the play produced, I didn't really know what I was doing. None of us did. There was little precedent to go on, though it was only natural that some of the terms of the Broadway agreements should serve as models for the off-Broadway agreements. We were making precedent for the future, and in the course of time the contract terms we used underwent changes that made them more suitable for the off-Broadway scene.

For example, established Broadway precedent called for the producer and investors in a successful play to share 40% of the income a playwright received from the sale of subsidiary rights—that is, income from a film or television adaptation of the play—if the play had run for twenty-one performances. The logic behind this was that the Broadway production of the play had contributed to the value of the play in other media.

Well, it was only natural as time passed that the playwrights' representatives would come to the conclusion that while an off-Broadway production does contribute to the value of the play in other media, it doesn't make the same kind of contribution that a Broadway production makes, and thus it would have to run for many more than twenty-one performances before the producer and investors got 40% of the author's subsidiary-rights income.

There followed a series of attempts to relate the amount of the share to the number of off-Broadway performances, until eventually a new formula became the established precedent: 10% to the producer and investors after twenty-one performances, 20% if the play runs for forty-two performances, 30% if it runs for fifty-six, and 40% if it runs for sixty-five or more.

Reasonable people, given a nonstandard situation, had found a way to accommodate the new circumstances and, in the process, developed a new standard.

WHEN TO BREAK WITH TRADITION

It's nice when precedent evolves naturally, as it did with the off-Broadway situation, old traditions serving as the models from which new traditions develop. But sometimes the old traditions and existing precedents prove to be so unsuitable that we have to break with them and create something new.

It happened rather abruptly in the theater, although it was quite some time in coming. Traditionally, authors and other creative personnel, as well as the producer, were paid a percentage of the gross weekly box-office receipts. Even in weeks when the play just made expenses, the star collected a handsome salary, the creative personnel and the producer got their royalty payments, and the investors got nothing. This could go on for years, and occasionally did. But as a consequence it became increasingly difficult to attract investors to the theater.

Something had to be done. The tremendous break with tradition came in 1977 with the abandonment of gross box-office receipts as the basis for royalty payments, and the adoption of a new system called the royalty pool.

It was a simple concept: the producer would take in all receipts, pay the fixed expenses and salaries but not the royalties, and then what remained—the net box-office receipts—would be divided among the investors and the royalty participants. The investors would receive 60-65%, and the remaining 35-40% would be shared by royalty participants in the same proportion that they formerly shared in the gross box-office receipts.

The new system has worked very well. When a play is doing good business, the creative personnel do much better than with a straight royalty. When a play does marginal business, they make less than they did before, but in the past they would have been asked to waive or defer their royalties anyway, to help keep the show alive. The royalty pool has now become the established precedent, and I suspect it will remain in place until it becomes obvious to anyone using their common sense that there is some better way to do it.

WHEN TO SAY YOU DON'T KNOW

Sometime you may be presented with the challenge of negotiating a matter that you know very little about, and when all you do know is that the usual procedure for finding out—doing research, making appropriate inquiries—is not going to give you sufficient knowledge to feel secure. I've described how we dealt with such a situation with *The Fantasticks*—developing contract provisions based on instinct and the overriding desire of all parties to see the play get produced. You can do the same thing when the subject under negotiation is something that nobody is very familiar with—involving a new concept, commodity or technology—or something that occurs so infrequently that only a very few people know how to deal with it.

Take what's happening in the multimedia and interactive technologies industries, for instance, new fields in which no one yet has a really firm grasp on what's going on. There are privacy issues and ownership issues and a hundred other issues yet to be resolved. Whole new conceptual structures need to be developed, entailing new law, new language, new contracts.

When Hollywood lawyers stuck language into their contracts whereby the studios acquired, among other things, the rights to the property on film, tape, etc., "and by any other methods not now known but hereinafter invented," they were trying to tie up all the possibilities. Many book-publishing contracts contained similar language, as did many recording contracts. But still there is a knowledge void: who really owns what rights in the new technologies? And how long should one have these rights? What should someone be compensated if their work appears on CD-ROM? a laser disc? etc.

There were, and still are, a lot of people who do not have answers to these questions but have to deal with them anyway. If that's your situation, you can hope that the person with whom you are negotiating is somewhat more adept in the field than you are. If that's the case, there is nothing wrong with saying, "You're the expert; what would be a fair deal?"

Will you be taken advantage of? It could happen, but probably not—because even though you may know too little about the subject to propose the deal yourself, you know when a deal that someone else proposes makes sense to you. And you know how to ask the other party to explain it if anything seems unclear. After the explanation, if the offer still seems wanting, speak up— or walk away. Even with your relative ignorance of the field, you must be given enough information to evaluate whether or not the deal is a good deal for you.

If you don't find yourself dealing with someone who knows more than you do and you're left to your own (albeit insufficient) resources, you have a couple of alternatives: you can wait until things become a bit more defined before making any deals. Or, you can plunge in and grope. You will know about as much as anyone on the subject, so just go ahead and negotiate for the best terms you can get; if it sounds right, make the deal. My advice is to try and make the deal for as short a period as possible, so you can take advantage of the new body of precedents as it develops.

Precedent is like an old shoe: if it fits, wear it, no matter how scuffed and worn-looking. If it sort of fits, stick in a new insole or stretch it until it's right. If no matter what you do, that shoe and your foot don't make a fit, toss it, get a new piece of leather and make a new shoe. (And if you can't tell a vamp from a sole, say so and call a cobbler.)

GROUND  RULE

PREPARE THE DOCUMENT

Since you have reached a critical stage in your negotiating, you might want to take a minute now to look at "Etiquette & Ethics II"—just to make sure you don't blow the deal accidentally.

Hypothetically, it shouldn't matter which of the negotiating parties actually prepares the written agreement— after all, you've worked and decided together on its terms, haven't you? But in fact it does matter, very much. So much so that, whenever possible, you want to write the document yourself.

There are many reasons for this, some obvious, some subtle. The most important one is that the party preparing the document can be selective about what to include. Although you do not want to intentionally omit an item of major importance to the agreement, a number of items may not have been discussed. Perhaps some items were glossed over as "boilerplate," or the parties assumed they were in agreement on them and didn't take the time to talk them through. Or one of the parties never thought to ask to include something that, if left out by the other party, the preparer, could accrue to the preparer's advantage.

For example, during negotiations about the granting and acquisition of the film rights to a novel, there may have been no discussion of the author's financial interest in a videocassette, if one is ever made. The attorney for the film company acquiring the rights could, without deceit or dishonesty, prepare the document making no reference to the sharing of income from a possible videocassette. If the author's representative doesn't catch this omission, the author could later lose out on a substantial source of royalty income.

Just as some items may be omitted when drafting the written agreement, others may be included that were never discussed, or their meanings may be shaded to better fit the preparer's point of view. Language is a powerful tool, and the person who selects the words that go into the agreement affects not only the content of the agreement but its tone.

Compare the wording and tone of these two contract provisions relating to a producer's paying for the playwright's transportation to the show's opening night if it opens away from the author's home. (1) "The author will receive a *per diem* of $150 and round-trip economy air transportation"; and (2) "The author will receive a *per diem* of $250, round-trip, first class air transportation for two and will be furnished with a limousine and driver for the rehearsal period until the day after opening night."

Since this provision is frequently overlooked during preliminary negotiations, its written form will set the tone for the negotiations about this provision—and perhaps about other contract items to follow—and can be taken to indicate what the producer hopes to end up with. Clearly statement 1 indicates a low-budget approach to the author and, you might speculate, to the overall production. Alarm bells may or may not ring when the author's representative reads this, depending upon the prestige and ego of the author.

Sometimes, even when you get to draft the agreement yourself, it's not easy to find the right language. As was mentioned earlier in the discussion about precedents, the person selling their life story for film or television may be reluctant to give the adaptor free rein in depicting their character and personality. The famous trial lawyer who is also a wife beater will probably not want to be depicted as a wife beater. But since many biographies are of interest to film and television producers for the sole reason that the person whose life is being told has done something unexpected, unpleasant, illegal or degrading, the preparer of the agreement is faced with a dilemma: how to word the document in such a way that it will protect the person who is selling his or her life story without hampering the freedom that a film or television producer needs.

We have seen that in almost every respect the preparer does stand to benefit from drafting the written agreement. And, in fact, *because* of this inherent advantage to the drafter, a principle of law has developed that you should keep in mind: if the court must resolve a question of interpretation about a specific contract item, it will usually interpret in favor of the person who did not draft the agreement; that is, it will interpret against the draftsperson.

Do not let this inhibit you from preparing the agreement, however. Remember: to create the document that sets forth the negotiated agreement is yet another way to influence the other party, to persuade him or her that your way is the way it should be done.

As was alluded to earlier, the first draft of a written agreement doesn't always include every issue that will end up in the final document—in fact, it rarely does. So you need to be ready to continue the negotiations beyond the first draft. But eventually the time will come when you and the other party think you have settled all the issues, and you can draft what you hope will be the final document.

As soon as you have written and reviewed the deal memo, informal agreement or more formal agreement (see examples in the appendixes), sign it and send it to the other party for his or her signature. And if, as a part of your deal, you will owe the other party money, be sure to include a check made out in the amount specified in the contract. In my experience, this offers the other party good incentive to sign quickly and not dawdle over the written agreement.

After a long period of negotiations for the film rights to a novel that my producer-client wished to acquire, the novelist's agent in London agreed to a contract which I then prepared. The contract provided for an option payment of $25,000, made payable to the agent. (Of course I included a letter instructing the agent to hold the funds in escrow until I had a fully signed copy of the contract back in my possession.) It seemed reasonable to assume that, with $25,000 in hand, a portion of which belonged to her, the agent would accept without a hassle several items in the contract that we had not discussed but which I wished to include. She did.

It should come as no surprise that if the bird in the hand is a big chunk of dough, most reasonable people will forgo the two in the bush.

GET THE MOST
(After All Is Agreed, Try to Get a Little More)

Once the negotiations have wound down, the deal is made, the written documents are being processed and you have no doubt that a good working relationship has been established, stop and think creatively once again. Now is the time to try for something extra that you might not otherwise be able to obtain.

When I'm at this point in the negotiating process, I turn to the other party and say, "No matter what happens, at this point we have a deal, and I would like to make a suggestion." Then I might add, "If you could see your way clear to adding another $5,000 to your offering, it would help my client considerably, and since you and my client are about to begin a long-term working relationship, helping her would also help you." I point out that while $5,000 is a drop in the bucket to a large organization like theirs, to my client it's a great deal of money, and such a small investment on their side would earn them a large amount of goodwill from ours.

Or, if it's a book deal and I've just finished negotiating the royalty my author-client will receive, I might try and get the publisher to agree to pay an increased royalty after some astronomical number of copies of the book have been sold. By that time they will have recouped their investment many times over, so they won't be hurting, and my client will have an added bonus in the event of skyrocketing sales.

As you can see from the above examples, my method of procedure at this juncture is to ask myself: "What can I ask for that will improve my position considerably while not affecting the other party all that much?" The answer frequently involves timing, as with the book-royalty arrangement: "What will benefit me at a time when the other party is faring very well?"

The progressive royalty arrangement, which we've worked out in the theater business, is another successful way to peg author's bonuses to the success of the show. It works something like this: when the investors recoup 100% of their costs, the author's royalty increases by a percentage point; when the investors recoup 200% of their costs, the author's royalty increases yet another percentage point; and so on. The percentages are negotiable, the point being that the author gets something more when the show is making money for everyone—and *only* when it's making money.

But it's important to point out when negotiating a progressive royalty like this that the request for a larger royalty is made not just because the producer and the investors are making more money and therefore should share some part of it with the author. Rather, the producer and investors are making more money because of the author's contribution, so it's the fair thing for the producer to do. And it's good business. When the producer wants to produce the author's next play, he will stand a better chance of getting the rights to do so.

Over and over in this book I've stressed the importance of building trust into the negotiating relationship, since that relationship is the prelude to a more important one—that of working together in the long term to achieve the goals of the agreement. And I can't overemphasize how a pleasant manner and a tone of voice that suggests but does not demand are key to building that trust and getting the most.

ETIQUETTE & ETHICS II

After the deal is made, while the written agreement is being prepared and during the discussion of the documentation of that agreement, you must take care to protect the relationship with the other party that you have so carefully built up over the period of your negotiations. By this time you will have established your credibility, reliability, honesty and integrity. You don't want to undo this through some careless mistake or behavior.

A few tips at this juncture might be useful:

- Even though the agreement is not yet signed, start acting as if it is a *fait accompli*. If you are hiring a person, stop looking for a different person for the job. If you are being employed, stop going on interviews with prospective employers. If you have agreed to sell your novel to a publisher, stop looking for a publisher. In other words, stop shopping around! Otherwise, there's a possibility that the other party might hear about your shenanigans and begin to think you are not 100% committed.

- Be aware of the line between friendliness and overfamiliarity, and do not overstep it with the other party. Of course, the location of that line will vary depending on circumstances and the sort of working relationship you are negotiating, but be attuned to it. For example, if you are negotiating an employer-employee relationship and you're the employer, is it appropriate for you to invite the person to drinks and dinner? It may not be. You need to know whether such conduct is proper, whether it will enhance the relationship or put one or both of you in an uncomfortable position. Proceed with caution!

- No matter what, if you are being represented by someone in the negotiations, and the other party is being similarly represented, you and the other party must avoid any discussion of the terms of the agreement. The two of you could easily misconceive some of the issues that are all settled and get into an unnecessary hassle over them. Let your representatives do the talking!

- Do not, under any circumstances, discuss your agreement with any friends, buddies, companions, acquaintances, enemies, relatives, associates, colleagues, strangers, pals, adversaries, foes or stray dogs. It is no one else's business, and if the party you are negotiating with has some of the same friends as you, the facts will end up distorted by the time he or she hears them, and there goes your relationship. After the deal is closed (and if it won't upset the other party), you can talk about it all you want.

Especially during this sensitive period, in the course of finalizing your agreement, keep the faith, but more important, keep your mouth shut. A blabbermouth's zeal can kill the deal!

LINING UP YOUR DUCKS: THE COMPLICATED DEAL

They say that politics is the art of compromise. The same is true about negotiating contracts—especially when there are multiple parties in the deal. If you are to make the deal happen, you must have all these "ducks" in a row. You must artfully maneuver them into line and get them to cooperate, not only with you but with each other. You must impress upon them that because there are so many of them, each wanting a part in the deal, each will have to make some concessions, each will have to compromise, or nobody wins and everybody loses.

Let me tell you about an incredibly complicated deal that I was asked to put together, one in which there were eight parties, all of whose cooperation we had to obtain if any one party was to get anything at all in the end. Even if you are unlikely ever to have so many ducks to line up in your own deal-making career, I think you will learn something from this experience of mine—and it was some experience!—because so many of the ground rules discussed in previous chapters were put into play here.

It all started when my client, a Broadway producer, wanted to acquire the stage rights to a very famous musical film. (I'd love to tell you its real name, but professional ethics do not allow it. Let's call it *See You in Miami, Mamie*). My client thought the stage rights were owned by a fast-developing, multifaceted film company which (to disguise its identity) we'll call "Torrid Productions."

I placed a call to Torrid Productions and confirmed that, indeed, they owned the film rights to *Mamie*. They suggested I make a proposal, which I faxed to Hiram Harmon, the attorney for Torrid. There followed a number of deliberate attempts by Mr. Harmon to evade talking with me: he was busy working on a corporate restructuring, he had to finish a film deal, his office was being painted, he was leaving the country for a month. You name it, he had an excuse.

During the two months this was going on, I became friendly with Bill Bowen, Harmon's associate. As I've mentioned earlier, it's always helpful to get to know people's secretaries and associates, and true to form, Bill prodded his boss until Harmon and I finally talked and agreed that we would make a deal.

Now, please don't think that because it only took two months to agree to make the deal, this meant we would agree on terms, get a signed contract and close the deal that quickly. No. It took six months to get an oral agreement from Harmon, and another year to get a signed written agreement—a total of eighteen months!

Now that some years have passed, I think I've figured out the reason for Harmon's delays. Most of us like doing what we know best, and it's a reasonable assumption that as the attorney for a major film company, Hiram Harmon was an expert in the law of film and television but not in the live musical stage business. It's also reasonable to assume that he would give top priority to those projects that were the most familiar and the easiest for him, and therefore put *Mamie* at the bottom of the pile.

In any case, while Harmon stalled, I was busy. Even though Torrid owned the film rights, there were a great number of other parties with some kind of an interest in the rights—including the heirs and assigns of the late Betty Brown, author of the short story, "Miami Tales," on which the Torrid Productions film was based—and we needed to get them on our side, too. Here they all are:

- The nursing home in San Antonio where Betty Brown lived before she died, and to whom she had given all of her assets when she went to live there, including the proceeds from "Miami Tales."

- Harvey Brown, son of Betty Brown, who, I was sorry to learn (because it would further complicate my life), had a lawsuit pending against the nursing home, claiming an interest in royalties from "Miami Tales." This meant that we could not obtain the rights until the lawsuit was settled or we had persuaded both sides to grant them to us (which, in fact, is what I did).

- Bob Mane and Richard Barton, the author and composer of the film, who had also written a play based on it. Although my producer-client did not want that version of their play because it was dated, Mane and Barton did have a continuing interest in the play, which had been assigned to the Wonder Licensing Agency, which handled the stock and amateur rights in the play and also represented Mane and Barton on other productions.

- CCM, the music publishing company, which owned five of the songs in the film, the five that just happened to be the most important, including the title number, "See You in Miami, Mamie." At the time of our negotiations, the most-often-used contract for the sort of Broadway musical my client wanted to produce provided the author, composer and lyricist with a royalty of 6% of the gross weekly box-office receipts. I shuddered to learn that CCM, too, expected a royalty—4% of the gross weekly box-office receipts. (Already I knew that obtaining financing for this production was going to be hard, but with this kind of a package it would be next to impossible.)

- Harry Deal, the award-winning playwright, who was hired to write the new, updated script of the play, which he would base on Betty Brown's short story and the Torrid Productions' film, as well as the original play by Mane and Barton. Things were not made easier when Deal, having finished the script, died, necessitating our redoing our contract with his estate, since dead authors don't have the cast- or director-approval rights that living authors have.

In addition to the parties named above, all of whom would require a share of the gross weekly box-office receipts, I had to factor in the twofold participation of my client, Lawrence Blake, who was to serve as both producer and director.

Here's what made me flinch when I sketched all this out on a piece of paper:

Torrid Productions	2.0%
San Antonio Nursing Home	1.0%
Harvey Brown	1.0%
CCM	4.0%
Harry Deal	2.0%
Mane and Barton (@ 2% each)	4.0%
Lawrence Blake (as director)	4.0%
Lawrence Blake (as producer)	2.0%
TOTAL	20.0%

At that time the chances of attracting investors in a musical play in which 20% of the gross weekly box-office receipts were already committed were next to impossible. What was I to do?

A *lot* of negotiating! Here's what each of the parties interested in *See You in Miami, Mamie* ended up with when all the contracts were signed:

Torrid Productions	1.0%
San Antonio Nursing Home	0.5%
Harvey Brown	0.5%
CCM	1.0%
Harry Deal	2.0%
Mane and Barton (@ 2% each)	4.0%
Lawrence Blake (as director)	1.0%
Lawrence Blake (as producer)	2.0%
TOTAL	12.0%

My chief negotiating strategy was to convince all the parties that unless each of them made concessions, no one would end up with anything. It took a long time and a lot of talking. I scheduled a lot of meetings and I said "please" a lot.

To start, my client Lawrence Blake agreed to reduce by 3% his royalty as director if the music publishing company CCM would do the same. CCM agreed to reduce their royalty by 3% only if Blake reduced his by the same amount *and* Torrid Productions cut theirs in half. Since Mane and Barton and Harry Deal were all members of the Dramatists Guild Inc., and the Guild controlled their contracts, we didn't have much flexibility about their royalties. That left only the nursing home and Harvey Brown. I explained to them that if each of them could prove that they owned what they were trying to sell, they could ask for the 1%; but since ownership was at issue in the lawsuit, they agreed to split the 1%, especially since all the others who could make concessions were doing so.

I made very clear to everyone that an unreasonable royalty demand was a deal-breaker; unless they were willing to reduce their royalties, the play would not get financing. When I presented figures to prove to the participants how much money was involved if the play was a huge success—and Broadway musicals are either huge successes or they close rather quickly—it became apparent that a lousy little 1% of the gross could amount to between $5,000 and $6,000 each week. A potential profit of $300,000 a year, not counting the subsidiary-rights income that might accrue, is nothing to sneeze at. This and my old adage, "2% of something is something and 90% of nothing is nothing," helped convince some of the parties to let up a bit.

The show must go on!

And it did. And it was a huge success.

Once I brought home to all the participants that unless everybody cooperated all would be lost, they were able to move forward. Once aware of their total interdependence, they could work together.

WORKING TOGETHER TO MAKE IT WORK
(It's Never Too Late to Change the Agreement)

Sometimes the best negotiations happen *after* the agreement has been signed, sealed, delivered and acted upon. Now that you and the other party know each other and can see how things are coming along and people are getting along, it's a lot easier to adjust the contract and fine tune the terms to better satisfy both of your needs.

You may find that you left something out of the initial agreement, or committed to some provision based on too little or the wrong information. Or you may just need to clarify some item that seemed perfectly clear when you first committed to it but now seems fuzzy and vague.

You may need to renegotiate in order to make it easier for one of the parties to comply with the contract provisions. It often happens that circumstances in general or somebody's situation in particular changes, making it necessary for everyone to make concessions. For example:

> A producer contracts with a lighting designer to design and execute a lighting plan using state-of-the-art laser lighting for a big Broadway musical. It's going to be sensational. Then the factory that makes the lights has a labor strike and cannot guarantee delivery in time for the opening. The producer and lighting designer must either delay the opening, gambling that the strike will be over in time to produce the special equipment, or sacrifice their innovations in

order to ensure some kind of lighting for the opening. In the end they renegotiate their contract to call for a new, more conventional lighting plan that does not include lasers.

Sometimes the request by one party for concessions by the other party turns out to be in the best interest of both parties—and perhaps others, besides. For example:

> A movie star signs a contract with a producer to perform in a play on Broadway. Rehearsals are to begin September 1 for an opening on October 7. After the signing but before rehearsals begin, the star is offered an important role in a film, with principal photography to commence September 15 and conclude by October 15. The star's attorney asks the Broadway producer to delay rehearsals until October 20 and the opening until November 27, and says that, in exchange, the star will agree to stay in the play for nine months instead of the customary six months.
>
> The producer can well see the advantage of having such a big star in his play for an extended period, but he's worried about his theater license, which stipulates an October 15 opening. The star's attorney decides to try negotiating with the theater owner, and discovers that the theater owner has an interim booking just waiting for a one-month limited run. He is happy to oblige the producer by renegotiating the theater licensing dates. In the end, *everyone* fares better.

Sometimes it may be good business and smart negotiating for one of the parties to initiate discussions in which they offer to make concessions they are not legally obligated to make. By voluntarily relinquishing some right, or granting the other party more rights, the "giving" party is making an investment in the goodwill of the continuing relationship. It's like giving out a marker that later may be cashed in.

I recently negotiated a contract with a television producer for an author-client of mine. The producer agreed to produce a television pilot which my client agreed to write, and the producer had successive options to produce ten more episodes based on my client's work. (An option gives the producer the right, but not the obligation, to acquire additional writings to be used for each episode.) This was a good deal for both parties. If the pilot was successful, the producer would pick up each option, one at a time, keeping my client busy writing television programs, perhaps for many years. If the pilot didn't succeed, the producer's liability was limited and he would not proceed with other installments.

It turned out that the pilot was a great success, and the producer picked up the option to do another episode, and then another after that. But then, because of other unrelated overcommitments, he ran out of cash and was unable to obtain financing for a fourth installment. When he approached me to say he couldn't produce any more episodes, I had a quick consultation with my client, who agreed to a deferred payment for the work he would do in writing the fourth episode and also for his work as script consultant and production consultant. In fact, the author went even further and agreed to actually waive the payments on the fourth episode if it turned out to be the last one produced.

I was friendly with the casting agent and the camera crew, and I asked them if they would agree to have part of their fees deferred so that the fourth episode could be produced and aired. They all agreed and the series continued. The deferred payments were made a year later, together with an unexpected 20% bonus for having waited for the payments and having run the risk of never being paid.

When the producer picked up the option to do two more episodes, it was time for me to collect the unspoken debt. My client was scheduled to receive payment for the fifth and sixth episodes in the following calendar year, but he really wanted to be paid in the current year so he could meet his tax commitments. When I asked the producer to accelerate the payments to help the author, he obliged without question. His cash flow had improved and he was happy to accommodate someone who had accommodated him. I cashed in my marker.

Working together, these two parties accomplished something that would not have happened had either party been intransigent. Had the author not deferred the payment for the fourth installment, there would have been no fifth and sixth installments. If the producer had not accommodated the author's request to accelerate his payments, he would have had an unhappy author unwilling to make any future concessions.

As it happened, the producer picked up all ten options and the parties are presently negotiating for a whole new series based on the author's work. This is a striking example of the benefits to be gained from working together to make a viable contract.

GOING INTERNATIONAL

Look at the names of the producers of the current Broadway plays and you will see the names of some big Japanese businesses. Look at my phone bill and you will see calls to Canada almost every day, to England almost every week and sometimes three or four times a week, to the European continent and Asia several times a month. My business, like every other business in the cultural arena, is increasingly international.

Just about everyone in every type of business these days is going to find themselves negotiating contracts and making deals in countries where they probably won't understand the language or be familiar with the customs and manner of conducting trade. Of course, you can always hire a local person to represent you—someone familiar not only with your particular type of business but with how to conduct that business in that particular market. And this is probably the best way to proceed if you intend to make a large number of deals over a substantial period of time; it will be worth the expense.

But how to proceed with the small deal, the occasional deal, the one-time-only deal? To the extent possible, by following the ground rules laid out in previous chapters. First—and always—be polite and attempt to build an atmosphere of trust between your negotiating partner and yourself. You will probably be dealing with someone who speaks English or has access to an English interpreter. (And by the way, don't assume that because you're talking with a Briton—especially a British barrister—that he or she and you are speaking the same language; British English and the British legal vocabulary can be just different enough to be dangerously confusing to an American.)

You can ask the other party to tell you about how a particular deal works in his or her country. A few years ago I was contacted by a small Japanese community theater that wanted to translate and present a stage version of the book *Cat's Cradle*, by my client Kurt Vonnegut.

I didn't have the vaguest notion of what a small theater in Japan might pay for these rights, so I asked the Japanese producer to send me what they would customarily pay for a limited noncommercial run. Kurt happened to be in my office when the letter from Japan arrived. It contained a one-dollar bill. I handed it to Kurt and he reached in his pocket to give me a dime for my share. I still have the dime on my desk.

When dealing with a Polish publisher, I didn't even have to inquire about the custom of the country; they told me right away how writers are compensated over there. Whereas in America a publisher gives the author a nonreturnable advance against royalty payments and then a royalty on whatever books are sold beyond the amount of the advance, in Poland, the publisher makes a single advance payment to the author for the right to publish and sell a specified number of copies of the book. For example, a payment of $5,000 may be made for the right to publish and sell 4,000 books.

Now, I couldn't think of a practical, *inexpensive* way to find out how many books the Polish publisher would actually print and sell. In fact, I couldn't even think of a practical, *expensive* way to find out how many books would be printed and sold. So I decided to take consolation in being offered any payment up front, no matter how unverifiable the print run or sales record. After all, until recently, many countries did not acknowledge copyright protection and have been notorious for printing books without paying anything at all. A payment up front was at least a step in the right direction.

Before you make a deal overseas, ask yourself the same questions that were presented in "Setting the Stage":

1. Will the party I am dealing with be able to do or deliver what I want?
2. What will it cost me?
3. What will I get?
4. What will I get on condition?
5. What must I do to satisfy the conditions?

You'll need to be a little more flexible and allow yourself a little more leeway with the answers than with a domestic deal. If you want to go international, it's necessary to take risks. Just see that you take care while taking them.

A FINAL WORD . . .

A composer and a book writer-lyricist I once represented wrote and composed a marvelous little musical for an off-Broadway production. For one reason or another they were not completely satisfied with the production, so they tried to fix it. The fixed version didn't quite meet their expectations, so they started major rewrites. They fixed and they fixed. Many months later, the newest version was less interesting, less inspiring and less creative than the original. Minor changes might have helped improve the play, but they had worked it to death. It went nowhere.

Another good friend and client wrote an inspiring television screenplay. Sure, it could have used some minor editing, but he was so unhappy with it that he tore it all up and started over again. The next version was still not what he wanted, so he did a major rewrite and then another, and yet another. The story lost its spontaneity. His screenplay was never produced.

While I wrote and rewrote this book, I was reminded of a wise lesson I learned many years ago from a painter-friend, Wolf Kahn. Wolf specialized in painting landscapes, but as a favor to my wife Annie and me he agreed to paint a portrait of our young daughter for a very modest fee. After three sittings spread out over about six weeks, we were invited to his studio to take a look at what he had done.

What a marvelous portrait! He had captured the essence, the spirit, of that sensitive twelve-year-old child. Wolf said, "You know, I could mess around with this for another five or six weeks and make a change here and there, but you have to know when to stop."

APPENDIX A

THE DEAL MEMOS

There are constant references in the entertainment industry to "letters of agreement," "informal agreements" and, especially, to "deal memos," a staple of the film industry in which the legal paperwork is particularly voluminous. I think people in other industries can make good use of the deal memo, so I've included a couple of examples here for your information.

Think of a deal memo as an easy way out, a way to enable you to get by with a short document when, for one reason or another—usually time constraints—a more formal agreement is not feasible. It is a very useful compromise when the parties have reached substantial agreement on the major items of the deal, but still have items left unresolved or not yet discussed. It's a way of "putting something in writing" until the full documentation can be prepared.

Often the deal memo includes a statement to the effect that a more formal agreement may be entered into later. But if that statement is not included, or if there is no subsequent formal agreement, the deal memo itself may constitute an enforceable contract.

If there is a dispute over a deal memo and a legal proceeding is begun, the judge or arbitrator may conclude that there is no contract because too many of the items that should make up the deal have not been settled on or written into the deal memo. On the other hand, the judge or arbitrator may complete the contract for the parties by deciding the items that are in dispute. This is more likely to be the case when both parties have already acted on the deal memo and are proceeding as if the contract is in effect—again, something that occurs frequently in the movie business, where final documentation may not be completed until the production process is well under way or, sometimes, until after the film is already made.

Deal Memo 1 outlines the terms of an agreement between Rome and Kraft, the writer and the producer of a musical play. It covers all the basics needed to get the book writing under way and stipulates when (see paragraph 4) the parties will enter into a more detailed contract, known as the Approved Production Contract for Musical Plays, which happens to be a fifty-five-page, single-spaced document.

Deal Memo 2 outlines the terms of an agreement between the American presenter ("MOD") and the sponsor of a London dance company ("PAG") for a series of dance performances in New York. It covers everything the parties need to firm up their plans for the performance series, but a more formal agreement would certainly contain a definition of net box-office receipts (which would require detailed negotiation concerning which expenses are deductible from gross receipts to arrive at net receipts). It might also contain the provisions for an obligation of the dance company to appear on television and radio for publicity purposes.

The sequence of documents included in Appendix C provides a third example of a deal memo. You might find it useful to compare this third example deal memo with the more detailed and more formal agreement succeeding it.

DEAL MEMO 1   **P.1**

1) Don Kraft (hereinafter referred to as "Kraft") does here-
    by engage Marty Rome (hereinafter referred to as
    "Rome") to write the book for *The Orange Grove*, a full-
    length musical play (the "Play") conceived by and to be
    produced by Kraft.

2) As the book writer, Rome agrees to work with Kraft, the
    conceiver, to develop the Play, and to cooperate and
    work with the composer(s), lyricist(s) and the director of
    the musical, when they are engaged. Rome agrees to
    deliver a treatment on or before December 31, 1995.
    Rome agrees to finish writing a first draft within ninety
    (90) days of receiving notice from Kraft that the treat-
    ment is acceptable and that he should proceed with the
    first draft. Rome agrees to finish the final draft within
    sixty (60) days after the first draft is returned to him by
    Kraft with suggested changes and with payment for the
    commencement of the final draft. Rome agrees that
    both the first and final drafts will be in manuscript
    form, double-spaced, and he agrees to furnish Kraft
    with two legible copies of such drafts.

3) Kraft agrees to pay Rome the sum of $2,500 upon the
    signing of this agreement, the receipt of which Rome
    does hereby acknowledge. If, after receiving the treat-
    ment, Kraft gives Rome notice to proceed to write a first
    draft of the Play, then, upon completion of the first
    draft and submission to Kraft, Kraft agrees to pay Rome
    an additional $5,000. Kraft agrees that he will make
    the determination whether to proceed to a final draft
    within thirty (30) days of receiving the treatment from
    Rome.

    Rome will deliver a final draft within sixty (60) days of
    receiving notice from Kraft to proceed with the final
    draft. Upon completion and submission of the final

draft acceptable to Kraft, Kraft agrees to pay to Rome an additional $2,500. Kraft will have a period of ninety (90) days from the receipt of the final draft to decide whether or not the final draft is acceptable to him.

4) The payments set forth above will be advances against a royalty in the amount of 1½% as set forth in the Dramatist Guild Inc. Approved Production Contract (APC). The parties agree that when the play proceeds to production, they will enter into an APC. In the event that there is a production of the Play and all of the royalty participants, including the Producer, agree to a reduction, waiver or deferral of the royalty payments, then Rome agrees to similarly reduce, waive or defer in an amount proportionate to the rest of the royalty participants.

5) Rome will receive substantial billing credit as follows: "Book by Marty Rome." Such billing credit will be in the same size, prominence, boldness of type as the type used for the composer and lyricist, and will appear wherever the name of the composer or lyricist appears.

6) If none of the material of Rome is acceptable to Kraft and none of the material is used, Rome will be entitled to no royalty and Kraft will have no further obligation to Rome of any kind.

7) Kraft will have a period of three years from completion of the book, music and lyrics (in no event later than five years from the delivery of the book by Rome) to produce a commercial production of the Play before a paying audience in accordance with the terms of the APC or, if the Play is produced off-Broadway or in a regional theater, in accordance with the terms of a contract to be prepared by Donald C. Farber or any other attorney then representing Kraft. If the Play is not produced within

the three-year period, Kraft may extend the option to produce the play for an additional one year by payment to Rome of a fee of $6,000 before the end of the three-year period.

8) If Rome becomes ill or dies before the final draft of the script is completed, and Kraft engages another writer to complete the script, then Rome's compensation herein provided will be proportionately reduced to the extent that a contribution is made by the other writer, it being intended that the allocation of payment to Rome and the other writer will be divided based on the number of pages submitted by each of them that are used in the Play as finally produced.

9) Any dispute or controversy arising under, out of, or in connection with this Agreement or the making or validity thereof, its interpretation or any breach thereof, shall be determined and settled by arbitration by one arbitrator, who shall be selected in New York City, pursuant to the rules of the American Arbitration Association. The arbitrator may award to the prevailing party reasonable attorneys' fees, costs and disbursements, including reimbursement for the cost of witnesses, including their travel and subsistence during the arbitration hearings. Any award rendered shall be final and conclusive upon the parties, and a judgment thereon may be entered by the appropriate court of the forum having jurisdiction.

Don Kraft

Marty Rome

Dated: September 1, 1995

Agreement, made as of August 1, 1995, between Modern Opera, Inc., a New York not-for-profit corporation (hereinafter referred to as "MOD"), whose address is 123 Western Avenue, New York, NY 10011, and Performing Arts Group (hereinafter known as "PAG"), whose address is State Theatre, 320 State Street, London, England.

WHEREAS PAG is the sponsor of a London dance company that they wish to present in New York City in the United States, and

WHEREAS MOD is knowledgeable in the presentation of modern dance and musical programs, and wishes to act as the presenter of the New York City production of the PAG dance company,

NOW THEREFORE the parties do hereby agree as follows:

1)   MOD has communicated with City Center in New York City with a view to arranging the presentation of the PAG Dance Company for the period between January 1, 1996 through January 7, 1996, and PAG agrees to deliver the talent to appear at City Center during that time. If it is impossible to book the City Center for the period between January 1 through January 7, 1996, MOD will make arrangements for another mutually agreeable time.

2)   MOD will engage professional promotional and technical staff, public relations and other personnel necessary to effectively present the PAG dance company in the City Center production. It is MOD's obligation to advertise and promote the production and to perform the services normally performed by a presenter of a dance company, including, but not limited to, the licensing and supervision of the theater; engaging and paying the orchestra; supervision of the personnel working in the theater, the

box office and other theater personnel; and the engaging
and supervising of promotion and advertising.

3)   The total budget, estimated to be $500,000, is to be
      paid by PAG to MOD to cover the costs of the produc-
      tion. PAG agrees to deposit $50,000 by telegraphic
      transfer on or before September 1, 1995, in the bank
      account designated by MOD in New York City. The bal-
      ance of the $500,000 will be paid as follows:

      On or before October 1, 1995 $100,000

      On or before November 1, 1995 $100,000

      On or before December 1, 1995 $100,000

      On or before January 1, 1996 $150,000

            The payments made by PAG to MOD will be
      used by MOD to pay for the rental of City Center; load
      in and load out; all staff living expenses and travel
      expenses of the company to and while in New York City;
      promoters; necessary union personnel and other inci-
      dental expenses necessary for the presentation, exclu-
      sive of the payments hereinafter specifically to be
      made by PAG.

4)   PAG agrees to deliver and pay for the professional talent
      for the presentation, including, but not limited to, the
      performers; directors; choreographers; set, costume and
      lighting designers; and the sets, props and costumes. It
      is the obligation of PAG to obtain and pay for all rights
      necessary to perform the musical works on the program.

5)   All net box-office receipts will be the property of MOD
      as consideration for the production and presentation of
      the PAG dance program. MOD may arrange and pay for
      a reception, and MOD will also be entitled to any net
      receipts from the reception, if arranged by them.

6)   The parties understand that, based on the commitment by PAG, MOD will be obligating itself to make payments to the theater and to production personnel, and that payment to MOD of the amounts as hereinabove set forth is an express condition of this agreement. With respect to the payments, time is of the essence.

7)   The parties acknowledge that this Deal Memo may be incorporated into a more formal contract. However, if there is no formal contract prepared and agreed and signed, this agreement will constitute a binding agreement between the parties.

Modern Opera, Inc.

by_____
    President

Performing Arts Group

by_____
    Secretary

APPENDIX B

SAMPLE LETTERS & AGREEMENTS

This appendix contains a performer's agreement, a collaboration agreement, and two letters of agreeement, all of which are samples of the kinds of agreements that are regularly used in the entertainment business. It is intended that these models can be adapted to the needs of your own business.

You may find it useful to compare the informal letters of agreement in this appendix with the slightly more formal deal memos in Appendixes A and C as well as with the even more formal agreement ("Option Agreement for *Always Faithful*") that concludes the sequence of documents in Appendix C. Regardless of the degree of formality, each type of agreement satisfies the requirements of the law and the needs of the parties for whom it was drafted.

PERFORMER'S AGREEMENT   P.1

Agreement between _____,
Producer, and _____, Performer,
entered into as of the ___ day of _____, 19__.

Performer agrees to perform the part of

_____ in the play_____

by_____

_____ for ___ performances on (dates)_____.

The play will be performed at _____.

As compensation in full, Producer agrees to pay and
Performer agrees to accept $_____ for each perfor-
mance of the play, the payment of which will be made
to the Performer on the day of the performance.
Employee is an independent contractor and as such will
be responsible for the payment of taxes, if any; Social
Security payments, if any; and any other such obligations. Performer acknowledges and understands that he
or she is working as such an independent contractor.

The Producer agrees to give the Performer billing credit
wherever the name of any Performer appears, and such
Performers' names will appear in alphabetical order in
the same size, boldness and prominence of type.

The Producer agrees to provide the Performer with
wardrobe necessary for the part.

Producer agrees to furnish the Performer with round-trip
transportation between New York City and the place of
performance. If Performer is required to stay overnight,
he or she will be furnished with appropriate accommo-
dations, that is, with food and lodging.

Performer acknowledges that he or she is being
engaged for a non-union production, and Performer rep-

PERFORMER'S AGREEMENT   P.2

resents that he or she is not a member of any performers' union, Actors' Equity or otherwise.

_____

Producer

_____

Performer

COLLABORATION AGREEMENT   P.1

Agreement made as of the 15th day of November by and between Elsie Crone ("Crone"), who resides at 2600 Elm Avenue, Hollywood, California, and Dora Dunne ("Dunne"), who resides at 1718 Oak Street, Los Angeles, California. Crone and Dunne are hereinafter referred to collectively as "the Collaborators."

WHEREAS Crone and Dunne wish to collaborate on the writing of a television series ("Series"), which will be written by them jointly and performed by them as co-authors.

NOW THEREFORE, the parties do agree as follows:

1) The Collaborators agree to cooperate in the development, preparation and writing of a show for series presentation on television in the Hollywood, California, area and elsewhere.

2) The Collaborators agree to cooperate as co-authors and as co-anchors in appearing and performing on the Series.

3) It is agreed that all writing and other artistic contributions to the Series created by Crone and Dunne will be owned jointly by them, and they will be the joint copyright holders of all such writings and contributions. Each agrees that she will not sell, lease, license or otherwise dispose of any rights of any kind in the Series without the express written consent of the other party.

4) The parties agree that in connection with the Series they will be equal in all respects. The parties intend to do business as a corporation, joint venture, partnership or limited liability company. The exact entity to be used will be agreed upon by the parties after consultation with the accountant for the business and the attorney representing the business. In all events, each of the parties will have an equal ownership in the business

COLLABORATION AGREEMENT   P.2

entity, and each will have an equal voice in running the business.

5) The parties agree to equally share all expenses and all income from the Series. If there are any salaries, fees, royalties, advances or other remuneration paid to either party in connection with the Series, the other party will receive the same salaries, fees, royalties, advances or other remuneration.

6) Each party agrees that she will not engage in any business that competes with the Series.

7) The parties agree to conduct themselves in a professional manner, to meet all deadlines and to appear as needed for television appearances and also for publicity for the Series. Each party agrees that she will not conduct herself in a manner that will disgrace or defame the Collaboration.

8) Each party hereby warrants and represents that their contribution to the Series is and will be original with each of them, except for any excerpts from copyrighted works which are specifically used with the written permission of the copyright owners.

9) This agreement is personal to the Collaborators and is not assignable by them, nor may any of the obligations imposed upon them be delegated, unless the other party consents thereto. Except as provided herein, this agreement shall inure to the benefit of the heirs, executors, administrators and assigns of each of the parties. This agreement shall not be subject to change or modification in whole or in part except by a written instrument signed by both parties.

10) Any dispute or controversy arising under, out of, or in connection with this agreement or the making or validity thereof, its interpretation or any breach thereof, shall

COLLABORATION AGREEMENT   P.3

be determined and settled by arbitration by one arbitrator who shall be selected in Los Angeles, California, pursuant to the rules of the American Arbitration Association. The arbitrator may award to the prevailing party reasonable attorneys' fees, costs and disbursements, including reimbursement for the cost of witnesses, including their travel and subsistence during the arbitration hearings. Any award rendered shall be final and conclusive upon the parties, and a judgment thereon may be entered by the appropriate court of the forum having jurisdiction.

11) The parties may at some future date enter into a more formal agreement containing the terms of this agreement, but if such more formal agreement is not entered into, this agreement shall be deemed to be legally binding and enforceable.

IN WITNESS WHEREOF, the parties hereto have executed this agreement on the date first above written.

_____

Elsie Crone

_____

Dora Dunne

DONALD C. FARBER

August 20, 1995

Phil Marx
123 4th Street
Anywhere, CA 97654

Dear Phil:

This letter, when signed by you, will constitute your agreement with Ted Copper concerning your design and supervision the execution of the lights plan for production by Mr. Copper of the play *No Way*, written by Jack Toby. As part of the development of the intended commercial off-Broadway production, the play will first be produced and presented by Mr. Copper in association with the Performing Arts Group, pursuant to the Actors' Equity Showcase Code, at the Showcase Theatre in New York City, on September 16 through September 20, and from September 23 through September 27, 1995.

In consideration of the services performed and to be performed by you, you are being paid the sum of $1,250, $250 of which constitutes payment for your work on the showcase production and $1,000 of which constitutes an advance against the payment which will

1928 FIFTH AVENUE NEW YORK, NY 10001 212.555.1234 FAX 212.555.1235

DONALD C. FARBER

Phil Marx
August 20, 1995
Page 2

be made to you if the play is later produced as a commercial production by Mr. Copper. In the event of such
later commercial production by Mr. Copper, it is agreed
that Mr. Copper will give you the option to design and
supervise the execution of the lights plan for such commercial production. Mr. Copper and you will negotiate
in good faith the terms and conditions of your employ-
ment as an employee-for-hire, but under no circumstances will the terms and conditions of such agreement be less favorable to you than the minimum terms
set forth in the contract of United Scenic Artists for a
lighting designer, applicable to the theater in which the
play is presented.

You will be given written notice of the commercial production and will have a period of seven days to respond
as to whether or not you will be available to work on
such production.

You will be given appropriate billing credit in connection with the showcase production and will be entitled
to purchase a pair of house seats at regular price for
each presentation of the play.

1928 FIFTH AVENUE NEW YORK, NY 10001 212.555.1234 FAX 212.555.1235

DONALD C. FARBER

Phil Marx
August 20, 1995
Page 3

If this meets with your approval, please sign the copy of this letter and return it to me so that I may have Mr. Copper sign and return it to you together with a check.

We may, at some future date, enter into a more formal agreement containing the terms of this agreement, but, if such more formal agreement is not entered into, this agreement shall be deemed to be a legally binding and enforceable agreement.

Sincerely,

/s/

Donald C. Farber

ACCEPTED AND AGREED TO:

_____ Dated:_____
Phil Marx

_____ Dated:_____
Ted Copper

1928 FIFTH AVENUE NEW YORK, NY 10001 212.555.1234 FAX 212.555.1235

DONALD C. FARBER

September 1, 1995

Dick Beard
456 7th Avenue
New York, NY 10036

Dear Dick:

I am writing to confirm our agreement in connection with our joint writing of a book based on the play *The Feast*. We have agreed to the following:

1) We will jointly write the book with me being largely responsible for furnishing the facts within my knowledge and editing, and you being primarily responsible for the writing of the book.

2) We will be equal partners except that you will be entitled to 60% of all receipts from all sources in connection with the sale, lease, license or other disposition of the book and all subsidiary uses thereof, and I will be entitled to the other 40%.

3) We will jointly own the copyright on the book, and we do specifically agree that there will be no disposition of any kind without the express approval of both of us.

DONALD C. FARBER

Dick Beard
September 1, 1995
Page 2

4)   We will collaborate on the writing and editing of
     the book, but since the major part of the writing-
     will be done by you, and since most of the facts
     will be supplied by me, if there is a dispute as to
     form or style, your decision will be final and
     binding, and if there is a dispute as to content,
     my decision will be final and binding.

5)   We will receive billing credit as joint authors of
     the book, and wherever either name appears,
     both names will appear in the same size, bold-
     ness and prominence of type. This provision will
     be incorporated into any contract entered into
     between us.

6)   Mike Dale is your representative in connection
     with the disposition of the book, and he will be
     paid by you in accordance with the terms of your
     agreement with him for the services rendered by
     him. I will represent myself in connection with
     my contribution to the book.

7)   Any dispute or controversy arising under, out of,
     or in connection with this agreement or the mak-
     ing or validity thereof, its interpretation or any

1928 FIFTH AVENUE NEW YORK, NY 10001 212.555.1234 FAX 212.555.1235

DONALD C. FARBER

Dick Beard
September 1, 1995
Page 3

breach thereof, shall be determined and settled
by arbitration by one arbitrator who shall be
selected in New York City, pursuant to the rules
of the American Arbitration Association. The arbitrator may award to the prevailing party reasonable attorneys' fees, costs and disbursements,
including reimbursement for the cost of witnesses, including their travel and subsistence during
the arbitration hearings. Any award rendered shall
be final and conclusive upon the parties, and a
judgment thereon may be entered by the appropriate court of the forum having jurisdiction.

I have tried to make this as concise and short as possible. If this meets with your approval and the approval of
Mike, your agent, to whom I have sent copies, I would
appreciate your signing and returning two copies to me
for my file.

I am sure that we will come up with a super book and
have some fun doing it.

Annie joins me in sending you our best wishes.

Sincerely,

/s/

Donald C. Farber

1928 FIFTH AVENUE NEW YORK, NY 10001 212.555.1234 FAX 212.555.1235

APPENDIX C

DOCUMENTATION FOR THE *ALWAYS FAITHFUL* DEAL

My intention with this final appendix is to provide you with a full picture of a deal in process. You may find it interesting to examine the entire sequence of documents relating to a deal that I made some years ago. Unfortunately, the real names of the parties involved and the play itself cannot be revealed here; suffice it to say, this was "a big deal."

I was asked by a producer-client to acquire the rights to a classic American play for presentation in New York—the "twist" being that it was to be performed by an all-Asian cast. The play had been written by one of the foremost dramatic playwrights in our history; hence, the executors of his will tended to be very possessive and wanted to make sure that any "unconventional" production would not diminish the overall dramatic value of this literary property.

It was necessary that we move rapidly, since one of the executors was very old and ill, and we had a rare chance to sign a prominent Asian director and a cast of Asian actors who possessed both great acting ability and good public relations value. After some preliminary telephone calls and faxes back and forth between the East and West Coasts, under the circumstances, I settled on a deal memo as the most appropriate and achievable form of agreement with the executors of the will. Later, after we had secured the most crucial elements of the production, I could prepare the more detailed formal option agreement.

Leading up to the deal memo that begins on page 134 are the letters of offer and counter-offer, which reflect the discussions in the preliminary telephone calls and faxes. After the deal memo, you will find the proposal, counter-proposal, and acceptance of royalty pool formula; the proposal of terms for the formal option agreement; and finally, the option agreement itself that concludes the sequence.

You will notice that the deal memo does not address certain important contractual elements—warranties and representations, indemnification, examination of the books, provision of house seats, limitation of competition—all of which and more are addressed in the formal option agreement. (To readily locate pertinent sections of this last document, see the agreement's Table of Contents provided on page 144.)

To help you keep everyone straight, here's the "cast of characters":

Bob Boyd, producer of *Always Faithful*
Donald C. Farber, attorney for the producer
John Jones, deceased playwright
Ted Erle, literary agent of the deceased playwright
John North, executor of the will of John Jones
Helen Hughes, executor of the will of John Jones
Milton Raines, attorney for the executors of
 the will
Lyle Chang, director of *Always Faithful*

OFFER

DONALD C. FARBER

April 13, 1995

Mr. Ted Erle
60 Ward Street
New York, N.Y. 12345

Dear Ted:

This will confirm our telephone conversation of today, wherein, on behalf of my client, Bob Boyd, I offered a $10,000 advance against royalties for the rights to produce and present, with an Asian cast, the play, *Always Faithful* (the "Play") by your deceased client, John Jones.

I suggested a royalty of 6% of the gross weekly box-office receipts, going to 7% after recoupment of the total production costs. We hope to tour the Play and pay the same royalty we will pay for the Broadway run.

Of course, John Jones will be given appropriate billing credit above the title of the Play, wherever the title appears, in type at least 75% of the size of the type used in the title. Provision will be made for a billing box.

The Executors of the Will of John Jones will have cast, director and designer approvals. Round-trip transportation between San Francisco, California, and New York

DONALD C. FARBER

Ted Erle
April 13, 1995
Page 2

City, for one of the Executors, Ms. Hughes, and living expenses will be provided.

Please respond to this at your first opportunity, as time is extremely important to my client.

With thanks and all best wishes.

/s/

Donald C. Farber

1928 FIFTH AVENUE NEW YORK, NY 10001 212.555.1234 FAX 212.555.1235

COUNTER-OFFER

Ted Erle

April 14, 1995

Mr. Donald C. Farber
Fax #555-1235

Dear Don:

In response to your fax of yesterday, the terms for the proposed Asian-cast production of *Always Faithful* are acceptable, except that the Executors are not willing to accept the royalty offer. My client, John Jones, was an author of exceptionally high renown, and his play has achieved the status of a classic.

If you can arrange for a royalty of 7% of the gross weekly box-office receipts, going to 8% after recoupment of the total production costs, the Executors will accept it. Since it is likely that we will ultimately move to a royalty pool arrangement instead of the percentage of box-office receipts arrangement, I hope that your client will accept this change.

Sincerely,

/s/

Ted Erle

60 WARD STREET NEW YORK, NY 12345

DEAL MEMO

Agreement made as of this 20th day of April, 1995, between John North and Helen Hughes, Executors under the Will of John Jones ("Owner"), c/o Ted Erle, 60 Ward Street, New York, NY 12345, and Bob Boyd ("Producer"), having his principal place of business at 345 East 48th Street, New York, NY 10013.

Whereas Owner owns and controls the stage-production rights to *Always Faithful* ("Play"), written by John Jones ("Author"), and

Whereas the Producer wishes to produce and present the Play with an Asian cast on Broadway in New York City, and the Owner wishes to grant such rights,

Now, therefore, the parties agree as follows:

1)   In consideration of an advance against royalties in the amount of $10,000, Owner does hereby grant the Producer the rights to produce and present the Play on Broadway in New York City with an Asian cast, to open on or before one year from the date of this agreement.

2)   Producer agrees to pay and Owner to accept during the run of the Play a royalty in the amount of 7% of the gross weekly box-office receipts until recoupment of the total production costs, and 8% of the gross weekly box-office receipts thereafter.

3)   The Producer has the right to do a pre-Broadway tour of the Play upon payment of the royalties hereinabove set forth, or upon payment pursuant to the terms of the royalty pool formula agreed to.

4)   After the opening of the Play on Broadway and during such run, upon payment to the Owner of

an advance against royalties in the amount of $10,000 the Producer may arrange for a first-class tour of the Play in the United States and Canada with an Asian cast. The royalty payable will be in the amount of 7% of the gross weekly box-office receipts until recoupment of the total production costs of the tour, rising to 8% thereafter, or in accordance with the terms of the royalty pool if a royalty pool is agreed upon. If the Producer is paid on the basis of a flat guaranty instead of a payment based on the gross weekly box-office receipts, the percentage payment hereinabove set forth will be based on the Producer's gross receipts from such tour rather than the gross weekly box-office receipts.

5) The author, John Jones, will be given billing credit above the title of the Play wherever the name of the title appears, in type at least 75% of the size of the type used in the title. If a billing box is used, the size type in the billing box will determine the size type used for the Author's name.

6) Owner will have approval of the cast, the director, the designer and all replacements thereof.

7) Producer agrees to furnish Helen Hughes, one of the Executors, with first class, round-trip transportation between San Francisco, California and New York City for the opening of the Play on Broadway, and agrees to pay her living expenses while in New York City for five (5) days prior to the official opening and two (2) days after the official opening.

8) The text of the Play shall not be changed in any manner, and Producer agrees that there will be no nudity in the Play unless specifically indicated in the script, and that nothing in the production

will alter the spirit or meaning of the Play as written.

9) The parties may enter into a more formal agreement containing the terms agreed upon and other mutually agreed-upon terms. If such more formal agreement is not entered into, this constitutes the entire agreement between the parties and is binding and in full force and effect.

10) There are no other rights being granted, including merchandising rights.

Executors under the Will of John Jones

by_____
John North, Executor

by_____
Helen Hughes, Executor

_____

Bob Boyd

PROPOSAL OF ROYALTY POOL FORMULA

DONALD C. FARBER

May 1, 1995

Milton Raines, Esq.
Fax #989-1234

Re: *Always Faithful* Asian Cast

Dear Milton:

We want to sign Lyle Chang as director, and in order to do this we must structure the royalty pool. We propose a royalty pool of nine (9) points for the author [owner], three (3) points for the director and one (1) point for the producer. These would be the only parties sharing in the pool, which would be 35% of the net receipts (gross box-office receipts minus fixed expenses), going to 40% on 150% recoupment of the production costs.

I think the author receiving $9/13$ths would be a good arrangement for your clients, but I need your approval before we can proceed. Since we want to sign Lyle right away, I would appreciate your prompt response.

With all best wishes.

Sincerely,

/s/

Donald C. Farber

1928 FIFTH AVENUE NEW YORK, NY 10001 212.555.1234 FAX 212.555.1235

COUNTER-PROPOSAL
FOR ROYALTY POOL FORMULA

MILTON RAINES

May 8, 1995

Donald C. Farber

Re: *Always Faithful* Asian Cast

Dear Donald:

In response to your recent correspondence, Lyle Chang is approved as director. We will want the following royalty pool arrangement: ten (10) points for author [owner]; 37 1/2% of net receipts, rising to 40% on 125% recoupment.

Yours sincerely,

/s/

Milton Raines, Esq.

313 PARK AVENUE NEW YORK, NY 10001 212.555.1237 FAX 212.555.0000

ACCEPTANCE OF ROYALTY POOL FORMULA

DONALD C. FARBER

May 11, 1995

Milton Raines, Esq.
Fax #555-0000
Re: *Always Faithful* Asian Cast

Dear Milton:

Your request concerning the terms of the royalty pool formula for *Always Faithful* is acceptable. I will incorporate the terms in the agreement with Lyle Chang, the director.

In the next few days, I will be sending you a letter suggesting additions that we should consider putting into a more formal agreement. In fact, I will be preparing such an agreement and sending it to you for your consideration. Unless you have some strong objections to the items contained in the letter I will be forwarding to you, I will prepare the agreement along the lines enumerated.

With all best wishes.

Sincerely,

/s/

Donald C. Farber

1928 FIFTH AVENUE NEW YORK, NY 10001 212.555.1234 FAX 212.555.1235

PROPOSAL OF TERMS FOR OPTION AGREEMENT

DONALD C. FARBER

May 19, 1995

Milton Raines, Esq.
Fax #555-0000

Re: *Always Faithful* Asian Cast

Dear Milton:

As I said I would do, I am faxing you a list of suggested items that I think we should consider in the preparation of a more formal option agreement for the Asian production of *Always Faithful*. As I said, I am in the process of preparing the Limited Liability Company Operating Agreement and Offering Documents, and want to present the most favorable terms possible to the prospective investors.

Will you please give consideration to the following:

1. Our option was for one year. Getting a director of the stature of Lyle Chang, whom we signed, and getting commitments for the kind of important Asian stars we are talking to, takes more time than we would hope. For this reason we would like to make provision for an extension of the option if necessary. We may want to wait to accommodate the schedule of a star or stars, and I am sure you would find this agreeable.

1928 FIFTH AVENUE NEW YORK, NY 10001 212.555.1234 FAX 212.555.1235

DONALD C. FARBER

page 2

2.   I would like to expand the warranties a bit. I know that we are dealing with an Estate, and this has its limitations, but it is possible to make some additional warranties to give the investors additional assurances.

3.   It would be most helpful if we could talk to the stars we are approaching about starring in a film as well as the Play. You were going to check out the film rights and let me know whether or not you have the rights. If not, we may be able to approach the owner of these rights, which would accrue to the advantage of your client as well as to mine.

4.   We want to spell out the royalty formula a bit more since we refined it in our negotiations with Lyle Chang.

5.   We could give consideration to my client producing other sit-down productions if the Broadway play is a success. This would involve some arrangement of exclusivity, in some areas at least.

6.   My client would like the opportunity to move the Play or produce it in the United Kingdom and Ireland, again if the Broadway production comes about.

7.   My client will want to arrange for a souvenir program and any other merchandising rights that

1928 FIFTH AVENUE NEW YORK, NY 10001 212.555.1234 FAX 212.555.1235

DONALD C. FARBER

page 3

your client would be willing to agree to.

8.   We should provide that my client can have the right to show fifteen (15) minutes on television or to read it on radio for exploitation of the Play, if there is no remuneration for my client other than his expenses.

9.   I think that an arbitration clause is good for both parties.

10.   I assume that the law of the State of New York would apply.

11.   You will probably want a provision for house seats.

12.   You probably want some kind of an agency clause.

So, given these few suggestions, please speak with your clients and get back to me as soon as you can conveniently do so. I am most anxious to get the offering documents completed so that we can get financed, and anything that you can do to speed this up would be most appreciated.

With all best wishes.

Sincerely,

/s/

Donald C. Farber

1928 FIFTH AVENUE   NEW YORK, NY 10001 212.555.1234 FAX 212.555.1235

OPTION AGREEMENT

OPTION AGREEMENT

FOR

Always Faithful

by

John Jones

TABLE OF CONTENTS

This AGREEMENT is made and entered into as of the 1st day of May, 1995, by and between the Executors of the Will of John Jones, deceased, as "Owner" whose address is 1001 Broadway, New York, NY 12345, and Bob Boyd as "Producer" for the purpose of producing and presenting the Play *Always Faithful*, written by the Author John Jones.

W I T N E S S E T H:

Whereas, Owner controls the rights in the stage play presently entitled *Always Faithful* (the "Play"), written by John Jones, deceased, and

Whereas, Producer desires to produce the Play upon the terms and conditions herein set forth, and Owners wish to grant him the rights,

NOW, THEREFORE, in consideration of the mutual promises and covenants herein contained, and other good and valuable consideration, it is agreed:

1. Representations and Warranties

To the best of the knowledge of the Executors, Owners warrant, represent and guarantee that:

(a) Owner, to the best of the knowledge of the Executors, is the sole Owner of the Play and that the same is original with Author and was not copied in whole or in part from any other work, nor will the uses contemplated herein violate, conflict with or infringe upon the copyright, right of publicity or any other right of any person, firm or corporation; and

(b) Owner has not granted, assigned, encumbered or otherwise disposed of any right, title or interest in or to the Play or any of the rights granted hereunder. Owner has the sole and exclusive right to enter into this Agreement and the full warrant and authority to grant the rights granted hereby.

(c) There is not now outstanding and there has not been any grant, assignment, encumbrance, claim, contract, license, commitment or other disposition of any right, title, or interest in or to the Play or any of the rights granted hereunder to Producer or by which the exploitation of the rights granted to Producer and the enjoyment and exercise thereof by Producer might be diminished, encumbered, impaired, invalidated or affected in any way.

2. Indemnity

(a) Owner will indemnify Producer against any and all losses, costs, expenses, including reasonable attorneys' fees, damages or recoveries (including payments made in settlement, but only if Owner consents thereto in writing) caused by or arising out of the breach of the representations or warranties herein.

(b) Producer agrees to be solely liable for all costs incurred in connection with any presentation of the Play and shall indemnify and hold Owner harmless from any claims arising therefrom.

3. Grant of Rights and Owner's Services

Owner and Producer hereby agree:

(a) In consideration of the sum of $10,000 as a nonreturnable advance against the royalty payments hereinafter provided, the Owner hereby grants to the Producer the sole and exclusive right and license to produce the Play and to present it as a professional Broadway production in the City of New York to open on or before June 1, 1996. Producer may extend the right to open the play on or before June 1, 1997, upon payment to the Owner of an additional advance against royalties in the amount of $10,000 before June 1, 1996. Although nothing herein shall be deemed to obligate Producer to produce the Play, Producer shall without limitation as to any other rights which may be granted hereunder, have the option to produce the play for an out-of-town tryout as a developmental production, at any time prior to the Broadway production.

-2-

(b) No script changes will be made without the approval of the Owner.

(c) Owner may attend rehearsals of the Play as well as out-of-town performances (if any) prior to the New York Opening of the Play.

4. Outside Production Date

Unless on or before the expiration of this option the Producer produces and presents the Play on the speaking stage in a regular evening bill as a paid public performance in a Broadway theater in New York City, Producer's right to produce the Play shall revert to the Owner.

5. Exclusivity and Continuous Run

The rights granted to the Producer are the sole and exclusive rights to produce the Play (the Producer may acquire an option pursuant to the terms of this agreement as hereinafter set forth to produce the Play in the British Isles and in the U.S. and Canada and on tour), and the Owner agrees that it will not, without the written consent of the Producer, which consent will not be unreasonably withheld, grant the rights to permit anyone to perform the said Play in any media within the United States of America, Canada or the British Isles, during the term of the option herein granted and the run of the Play, or during the period that the Producer retains any rights or option to produce the Play anywhere in the United States, Canada or the British Isles.

If the Play is produced within the option period herein granted, the exclusive right to produce each production of the Play shall continue during each such production's continuous run. Each said production of the Play shall be deemed closed (that is, the continuous run shall have terminated) if no paid performances have been given for such production for a period of eight (8) weeks. After the Play has closed and after all options to produce the Play have expired, all rights shall revert to the Owner subject to any other terms specifically herein set forth.

6. Consideration

(a) The Owner will be paid either a royalty of seven percent (7%) of the gross weekly box-office receipts until recoupment of 100% of the total production costs and eight percent (8%) of the gross weekly box-office receipts thereafter, or

(b) If the other royalty participants agree to be paid in accordance with a royalty pool formula, then the Owner agrees that the aforesaid advance payments shall be against royalties payable in accordance with a royalty pool formula as follows:

(1) "Net Receipts" for the purpose of this formula shall mean all gross weekly box-office receipts less all customary and reasonable expenses except those variable expenses payable to royalty participants as part of this formula.

(2) "Royalty Pool" for the purpose of this formula shall mean the share of the Net Receipts allocated to the royalty participants.

(3) "Net Profits" for the purpose of this formula shall mean Net Receipts less the amount of the Royalty Pool.

(4) All royalty participants and the Producer for the producer's fee will share the Royalty Pool, which shall be 35% of the Net Receipts. The remaining 65% of the weekly Net Receipts, the Net Profits, will be paid to the limited partnership until 125% of the total production costs of the Play are recouped and the royalty participants will thereafter share 40% of the weekly Net Receipts. The royalty participants and the Producer for the producer's fee are each allocated a certain number of points for their respective contributions to the Play.

(5) The royalty participants' share of the Royalty Pool will be based on the following division:

	Points
Executors of John Jones, as Owner of rights	10.0
Producer's fee	2.0

-4-

Director	3.0
Designers and Choreographer (Estimated)	1.0

Each royalty participant will receive a minimum weekly royalty in the amount of $750 for each one point allocated to such respective party. The minimum weekly royalty will be paid to the royalty participants weekly, and the balance to which the royalty participants are entitled from the royalty pool will be paid based on a four-week average of the net receipts and will be paid within one week after each four-week period. The total points payable to all Royalty Pool participants will not exceed eighteen (18) points.

(6) What amount the theater will be paid will be determined by negotiations, but it is anticipated that the theater will be paid a fixed fee each week and may also receive a percentage of the gross weekly box-office receipts. The payment to the theater will be considered an expense that is deducted prior to the division of the weekly Net Receipts, as above set forth, between royalty participants and the production company, whether it is a fixed amount or a percentage of the gross weekly box-office receipts or a combination of both. The Net Profits of the limited liability company represented by the 65% of the weekly Net Receipts will first be used to repay the investors their capital contributions, and thereafter the weekly Net Profits will be equally split with the limited partners receiving 50% and the Producer receiving 50%.

7. Computation of Royalties

"Gross weekly box-office receipts" shall be computed in the manner determined by the League of American Theatres, provided, however, that in making such computation there shall be deducted: (a) any federal admission taxes; (b) any commissions paid in connection with theater parties or benefits; (c) those sums equivalent to the former five (5) percent New York City Amusement Tax, the net proceeds of which are set aside in pension and welfare funds in the theatrical unions and ultimately paid to said funds; (d) commissions paid in connection with automated ticket distribution or remote box offices, e.g., Ticketron (but not ticket brokers) and any fees paid or discounts allowed in connection with credit-card sales; (e) subscription fees; (f) discounts provided to any discount ticket service (e.g. TDF); and (g) for "BROADWAY CARES" if other royalty participants similarly agree to this deduction.

8. Traveling Expenses and *Per Diem*

If either Executor of the Will of John Jones is required outside a 150-mile radius of his home during rehearsals, he or she will be furnished with first-class, round-trip transportation and will be paid hotel and travel expenses in the amount of $200 per day during the period that he or she is away from home.

9. Tours

Provided that Producer has produced and presented the Play hereunder on Broadway in New York City for twenty-one (21) consecutive, paid, public performances or more, including in this computation no more than seven (7) paid previews immediately consecutive to the opening, the Producer shall have the option to produce the Play for a first-class tour or for a "bus and truck" tour. Producer must exercise this option within six (6) months after the official opening of the Play in New York City by giving Owner notice in writing accompanied by the payment of the following:

(a) If the tour is to be a first-class tour, a nonreturnable advance against the royalties as provided in Article X of the Dramatists Guild, Inc. Approved Production Contract ("APC"), and the royalty for such tour shall be as provided in Article IV of the APC, or

(b) If the tour is to be a "bus and truck" tour, a nonreturnable advance against the royalties in the amount of $5,000, for the rights to open the first presentation of the tour

-6-

within twelve (12) months of the receipt of notice by the Owner. The Producer may extend the right to open the Play during an additional six (6) months after the expiration of the twelve-month period if the Producer gives the Owner notice in writing before the termination of the said twelve months, together with a further advance payment against the royalties in the amount of $5,000, and the Producer has engaged a star or director in consultation with and subject to the approval of the Owner, which approval will not be unreasonably withheld. The royalties for the "bus and truck" tour shall be computed in the same manner that the royalties are computed as provided in the royalty pool formula set forth in paragraph 6 of this agreement.

10. Other Productions

If the Play produced hereunder runs for twenty-one (21) consecutive paid public performances, including no more than seven (7) previews immediately consecutive to the opening in New York City, then the Producer shall have the option to produce successive sit-down productions in the United States and Canada. To exercise this option, within six (6) months after the official opening of the Play in New York City, Producer must give the Owner notice in writing of the city or cities for the first production, accompanied by a check in the amount of $5,000 as a nonreturnable advance against royalties for the first such sit-down production and open the Play within six months of receipt of such notice. The first sit-down production, as well as all subsequent sit-down productions, may run concurrently in two or more locations.

Within six (6) months after the close of the last performance of each successive sit-down production, the Producer may give successive options to produce sit-down productions and in each case must make a payment of a nonreturnable advance against the royalties in the amount of $5,000 for each such respective production and open the Play within six (6) months of receipt of such notice.

-7-

Producer may extend each option to open the Play for an additional six (6) months upon payment of an additional $5,000 fee, within the first six (6)-month period.
The royalties payable for each sit-down production shall be as provided in the royalty pool formula set forth in paragraph 6 of this agreement.

11. Production in the United Kingdom and Ireland

If the Producer has produced the Play in New York for not less than twenty-one (21) consecutive paid public performances, including no more than seven (7) previews immediately consecutive to the opening, Producer shall have the exclusive right to produce the Play on the speaking stage in the United Kingdom and Ireland upon all the terms and conditions which apply to a New York production, to open at any time up to and including one (1) year after receipt of notice from the Producer, which notice must be given within ninety (90) days from the New York City opening. Together with such notice the Producer must make payment to the Owner of:

(a) If the production is for a first-class production on the West End in London, the advance provided for and the royalties payable shall be in the amounts as set forth in the APC, and,

(b) If the production is for other than a first-class production on the West End in London, Producer shall pay the Owner an amount as follows:

(1) A nonreturnable advance against the royalty payment in the amount of $2,500 if the production is in a theater of 299 seats or less, and

(2) $3,500 if the proposed production is in a theater of more than 299 seats. The royalties payable for other than a first-class West End production shall be 7% of the gross weekly box-office receipts until the total production costs are recouped and 8% thereafter.

-8-

Producer may produce the Play in association with or under lease to a British or Irish producer. In such case Producer's obligation to make the royalty payments herein provided shall remain unimpaired. If it is to be produced on the West End in London, such contract between Producer and the British producer shall require the Play to be produced under the same terms as would apply if the original New York production had been produced under the Approved Production Contract for a first-class production.

12. _Force Majeure_

If Producer shall be prevented from exercising any option hereunder, or if any production of the Play hereunder shall be prevented or interrupted due to epidemic, fire, action of the elements, strikes, labor disputes, governmental order, court order, act of God, public enemy, wars, riots, civil commotion, illness or any other similar cause beyond the Producer's control, such prevention or interruption shall not be deemed a breach of this agreement or a cause for forfeiture of Producer's rights hereunder, and the time for exercise of such option and/or the time by which the first paid public performance must take place shall be extended for the number of days during which the exercise of such option or presentation of such production was prevented; provided that if a failure to exercise any option or any prevention or interruption of production due to any such cause shall continue for sixty (60) days, then Owner shall have the right to terminate Producer's production rights for the interrupted run or terminate Producer's right to exercise such option (as the case may be) by written notice to Producer.

13. Approvals and Changes

No change in the Play will be made without the approval of Owner. Such changes shall become the property of Owner.

Owner shall have approval of the cast, understudies, director and designers, as well as replacements of any of the above.

14. Accounting

Within seven (7) days after the end of each production week Producer agrees to forward to Owner the amounts due as compensation for such week and also, within such time, to furnish box-office statements of each performance of the Play during such week, signed by the treasurer or treasurers of the theater in which performances are given, and countersigned by Producer or his duly Ownerized representative. Box-office statements and payments due for productions presented more than five hundred (500) miles from New York City may be furnished and paid within fourteen (14) days after the end of each week, and for productions presented in the United Kingdom or Ireland, within twenty-five (25) days. Owner's agent will be sent copies of all financial statements forwarded to investors and with a statement of the monthly operating expenses as they become available.

15. Billing Credits

In all programs, house boards, painted signs and paid advertising of the Play under the control of Producer (except marquees, ABC and teaser ads and small ads where no credits are given other than to the title of the Play, the name(s) of the star(s) if any, the name of the theater and/or one or more critics' quotes), credit shall be given to John Jones, as Author.

The name of John Jones, as Author, shall be in type at least 75% of the size, boldness and prominence of the title of the Play. No names except the title of the Play and a star(s) shall be more prominent than the Author's name, and no names other than the Producer's shall appear above that of the Author.

Wherever credits are accorded in connection with the Play in a so-called "billing box" pursuant to which the Author is entitled to credit, the size of both the Author's and Producer's credits shall be determined by the size of the title of

-10-

the Play in such "billing box" and will appear only in the billing box.

No inadvertent failure to accord the billing herein provided shall be deemed a breach hereof, unless the same shall not be remedied promptly upon written notice from Owner to Producer.

16. House Seats

Producer shall hold two (2) pair of adjoining house seats for Owner or his designee, for all performances of the Play in New York City in the first ten (10) rows in the center section of the orchestra. Additionally, Owner shall have the right to purchase four (4) additional pair of seats in good locations for Opening Night. Such house seats shall be held forty-eight (48) hours prior to the scheduled performance and shall be paid for at the regularly established box-office prices. Owner acknowledges and agrees that the theater tickets made available hereunder cannot, except in accordance with the regulations promulgated by the office of the Attorney General of the State of New York, be resold at a premium or otherwise, and that complete and accurate records will be maintained by them, which may be inspected at reasonable times by a duly designated representative of Producer and/or the Attorney General of the State of New York, with respect to the disposition of all tickets made available hereunder.

17. Radio and Television Exploitation

Producer shall have the right to authorize one or more radio and/or television presentations of excerpts from Producer's production of the Play (each such presentation not to exceed fifteen (15) minutes) for the sole purpose of exploiting and publicizing the production of the Play, including presentation on the Antoinette Perry Award (Tony) television program and similar award programs, provided Producer receives no compensation or profits (other than reimbursement for out-of-pocket expenses), directly or indirectly, for authorizing such radio or television presentations.

-11-

18. Right of Assignment

Producer shall have the right to assign this Agreement to a Limited Liability Company in which Producer or an entity controlled by Producer is a managing member; to a joint venture in which either Producer is one of the joint venturers; or to a corporation in which the Producer is the controlling principal. Any other assignments will require the Owner's approval in writing.

19. Ownership of Copyright and Ideas Contributed by Third Parties

The Executors of the Will of John Jones, as Owner of the Play, shall control the uses and disposition of the Play except as otherwise provided hereunder. All rights in and to the Play not expressly granted to Producer, hereunder are hereby reserved to Owner for use and disposition. All ideas with respect to the Play, contributed by any Producer, shall belong to Owner. Producer shall not make any representations to any third party that any ideas contributed or to be contributed by such third party to the Play belong to anyone other than the Owner. Any copyright of the Play, including any extensions or renewals thereof throughout the world, shall be in the name of the Owner.

20. Notices

Any notice to be given hereunder shall be sent by registered or certified mail, return receipt requested, or telegraph or cable addressed to the parties at their respective addresses given herein, or by delivering the same personally to the parties at the addresses first set forth herein. Any party may designate a different address by notice so given. Copies of all notices shall be sent to: Donald C. Farber, Farber Rich & Simmons, LLP, 1928 Fifth Avenue, New York, New York 10001.

23. Arbitration

Any dispute or controversy arising under, out of, or in connection with this Agreement or the making or validity

-12-

thereof, its interpretation or any breach thereof, shall be determined and settled by arbitration by one arbitrator who shall be selected by mutual agreement of the parties hereto, in New York City, pursuant to the rules of the American Arbitration Association. The arbitrator is Ownerized to award to the prevailing party reasonable attorneys' fees, costs and disbursements, including reimbursement for the cost of witnesses, travel and subsistence during the arbitration hearings. Any award rendered shall be final and conclusive upon the parties and a judgment thereon may be entered by the appropriate court of the forum having jurisdiction.

24. Applicable Law, Entire Agreement

This Agreement shall be deemed to have been made in New York, New York and shall be governed by New York law applicable to agreements duly executed and to be performed wholly within the State of New York. This Agreement shall be the complete and binding agreement between the parties and may not be amended except by an agreement in writing signed by the parties hereto.

25. Successors and Assigns

The terms and conditions of this Agreement shall be binding upon the respective executors, administrators, successors and assigns of the parties hereto, provided, however, that none of the parties hereto shall, except as otherwise herein provided, have the right, without the written consent of the parties, to assign his or her rights or obligations hereunder, except the right to receive the share of the proceeds, if any, from the Play, payable to such party hereunder.

It is acknowledged that the Executors of the Will of John Jones are the Owner and Bob Boyd is the Producer of the Play. This agreement is entered into with the knowledge that it will be assigned by Producer, to a Limited Liability Company to be formed, which will enjoy all of the benefits and will assume all of the obligations of the Producer hereunder. It is also acknowledged that there may be parties other than, and in addition to Bob Boyd, who will be producers who will be bound by the terms of this agreement.

IN WITNESS WHEREOF, the parties hereto have hereunto set their hands as of the day and year first above written.

_____

John North, Executor of the Will of John Jones

_____

Helen Hughes, Executor of the Will of John Jones

_____

Bob Boyd, Producer

ABOUT THE AUTHOR

Donald C. Farber has an active theatrical practice in New York City and other parts of the U.S. and world. He represents many theatrical productions, actors, directors, producers, authors, theater owners, repertory companies, and persons in every aspect of the theater, film, and other creative arts. He is a member of the law firm Farber Rich & Simmons, LLP.

Mr. Farber is the author of six books dealing with various business and legal aspects of theater. His latest, *The Amazing Story of The Fantasticks, America's Longest Running Play* (Citadel Press, 1991), is a complete story of the making of the musical play that he helped put together in 1960. Other titles include: *From Option to Opening: A Guide to Producing Plays Off Broadway* (Limelight Editions, 1993); *Producing Theatre: A Comprehensive Legal and Business Guide* (Limelight Editions, 1990); *Producing, Financing and Distributing Film* (Limelight Editions, 1972); and *Actor's Guide: What You Should Know About the Contracts You Sign* (DBF Publications, 1971). He is the General Editor of *Entertainment Industry Contracts: Negotiating and Drafting Guide* (Matthew Bender, updated three times yearly).

Donald Farber resides in New York City with his wife Ann.